Microsoft®

FrontPage 2000
Step by Step

ActiveEducation™

Microsoft Press

One Microsoft Way
Redmond, Washington 98052-6399

Library of Congress Cataloging-in-Publication Data
Microsoft FrontPage 2000 Step by Step / ActiveEducation, Inc.
       p.   cm.
      Includes index.
      ISBN 1-57231-980-1
      1. Microsoft FrontPage. 2. Web sites--Design. 3. Web publishing.
  I. ActiveEducation, Inc.
 TK5105.8885.M53M535 1999
 005.7'2--dc21   98-48189
                                CIP
Printed and bound in the United States of America.

1 2 3 4 5 6 7 8 9 WCWC 4 3 2 1 0 9

Distributed in Canada by ITP Nelson, a division of Thomson Canada Limited.

A CIP catalogue record for this book is available from the British Library.

Microsoft Press books are available through booksellers and distributors worldwide. For further information about
international editions, contact your local Microsoft Corporation office. Or contact Microsoft Press International directly
at fax (425) 936-7329. Visit our Web site at mspress.microsoft.com.

For ActiveEducation, Inc.
Managing Editor: Ron Pronk
Project Editor: Kate Dawson
Writer: Scott Palmer
Production/Layout: Katherine Stark
Technical Editors: Amy Carpenter, Rebecca Van Esselstine,
  Patrick Vincent
Indexer: Jenifer F. Walker
Proofreader: Holly Freeman

For Microsoft Press
Acquisitions Editor: Susanne M. Forderer
Project Editor: Jenny Moss Benson

Contents

QuickLook Guide

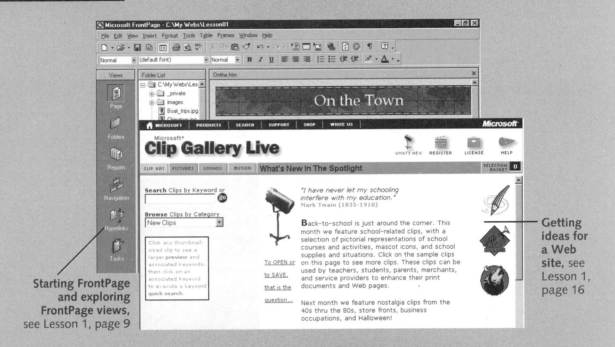

Starting FrontPage and exploring FrontPage views, see Lesson 1, page 9

Getting ideas for a Web site, see Lesson 1, page 16

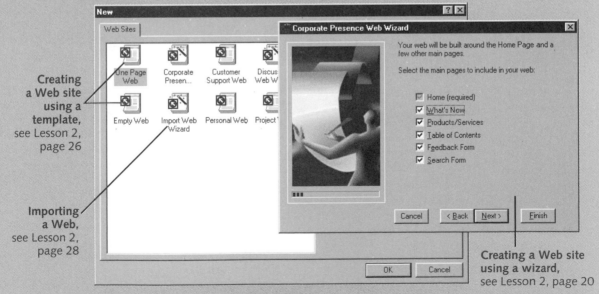

Creating a Web site using a template, see Lesson 2, page 26

Importing a Web, see Lesson 2, page 28

Creating a Web site using a wizard, see Lesson 2, page 20

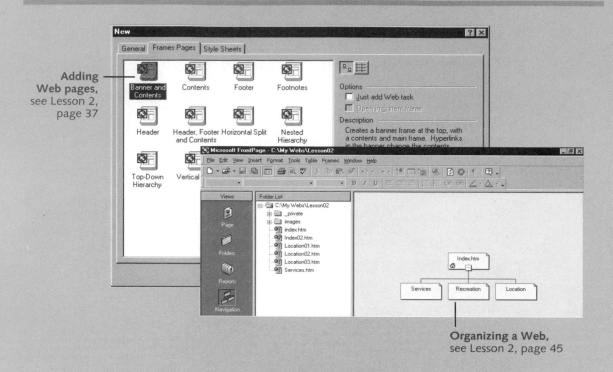

Adding Web pages, see Lesson 2, page 37

Organizing a Web, see Lesson 2, page 45

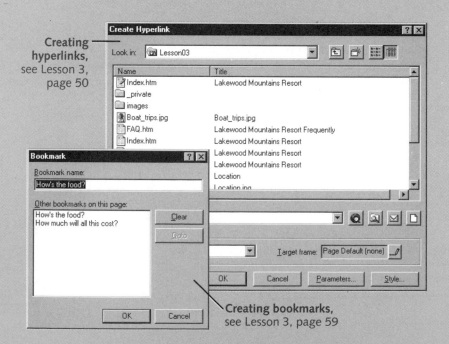

Creating hyperlinks, see Lesson 3, page 50

Creating bookmarks, see Lesson 3, page 59

Using components, see Lesson 4, page 84

Using themes, see Lesson 4, page 78

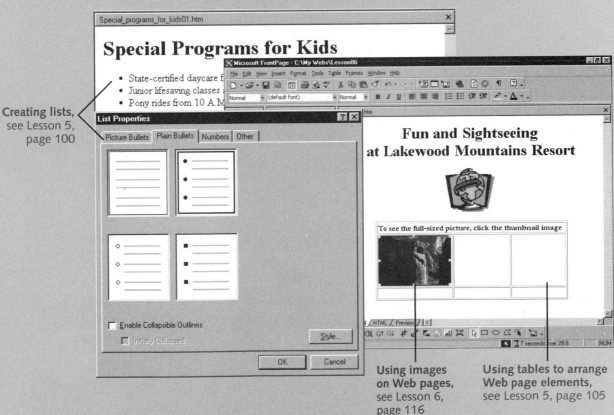

Creating lists, see Lesson 5, page 100

Using images on Web pages, see Lesson 6, page 116

Using tables to arrange Web page elements, see Lesson 5, page 105

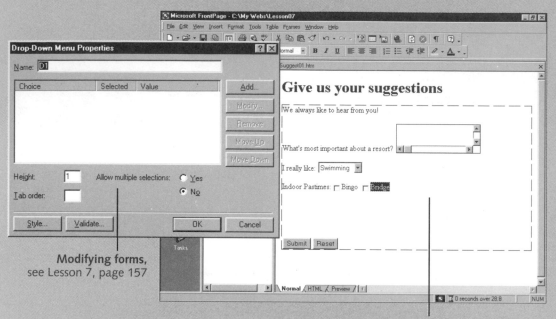

Modifying forms,
see Lesson 7, page 157

Creating forms,
see Lesson 7, page 147

**Using shared borders
and navigation bars,**
see Lesson 8, page 182

Creating frames pages,
see Lesson 8, page 172

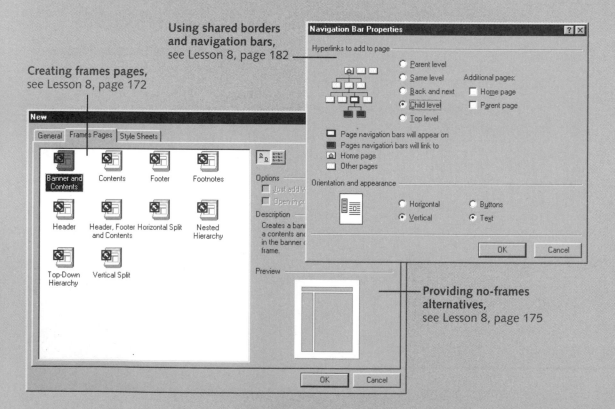

**Providing no-frames
alternatives,**
see Lesson 8, page 175

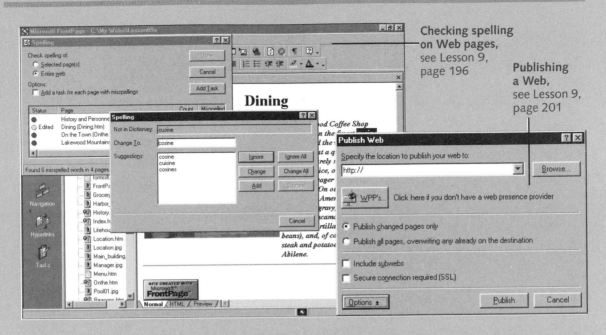

Checking spelling on Web pages, see Lesson 9, page 196

Publishing a Web, see Lesson 9, page 201

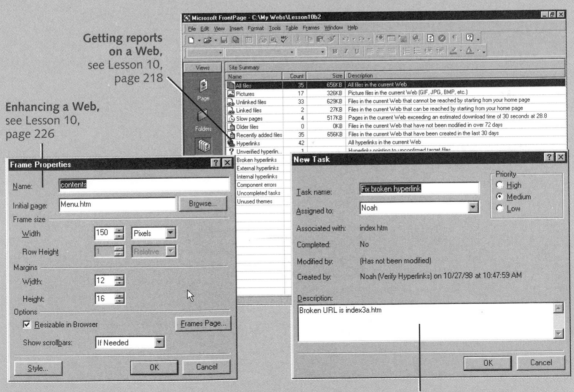

Getting reports on a Web, see Lesson 10, page 218

Enhancing a Web, see Lesson 10, page 226

Managing FrontPage tasks, see Lesson 10, page 222

Finding Your Best Starting Point

Microsoft FrontPage 2000 is the newest Microsoft Web design tool for personal computers. FrontPage 2000 expands the foundation of FrontPage 98 to allow you to take full advantage of the latest developments in Web technology. Whether you're designing a Web for your job, for your personal interests, or both, you will find that FrontPage 2000 is efficient, fast, and reliable. With *Microsoft FrontPage 2000 Step by Step,* you will quickly and easily learn how to use FrontPage 2000.

Finding Your Best Starting Point in This Book

This book is organized for beginning Web designers, as well as readers who have had experience with these types of programs and are switching or upgrading their current Web design tool to FrontPage 2000. Use the following tables to find your best starting point in this book.

If you are	Follow these steps
New	
To computers, Windows, or Microsoft FrontPage	❶ Install the practice files as described in "Using the Microsoft FrontPage 2000 Step by Step CD-ROM."
	❷ Become aquainted with the Windows operating system and how to use the online Help system by working through Appendix C, "If You're New to Windows."
	❸ Learn basic skills for using Microsoft FrontPage 2000 by working through Lessons 1 through 3.

If you are	Follow these steps
New To Web design	**1** Install the practice files as described in "Using the Microsoft FrontPage 2000 Step by Step CD-ROM." **2** Work through Lessons 1-3 in sequence. **3** Work through Lessons 4-10 as needed.

If you are	Follow these steps
Switching From a different Web design tool	**1** Install the practice files as described in "Using the Microsoft FrontPage 2000 Step by Step CD-ROM." **2** Skim through Lesson 1 to review basic Web design concepts. **3** Work through Lessons 2-10 in sequence to learn the FrontPage approach to Web design.

If you are	Follow these steps
Upgrading From FrontPage 98	**1** Install the practice files as described in "Using the Microsoft FrontPage 2000 Step by Step CD-ROM." **2** Skim through Lessons 1 and 2 to review basic Web design concepts and learn about some of the new features in FrontPage. **3** Work through Lesson 6 to learn how FrontPage 2000 allows you to place items in precise locations on a Web page by using CSS positioning. **4** Work through the other lessons as needed to review FrontPage and learn about other new features.

If you are	Follow these steps
Referencing This book after working through the lessons	**1** Use the index to locate information about specific topics, and use the Table of Contents to locate information about general topics. **2** Read the Quick Reference at the end of each lesson for a brief review of the major topics in the lesson. The Quick Reference topics are presented in the same order as the topics are presented in the lesson.

New Features in FrontPage 2000

The following table lists the major new features of FrontPage 2000 covered in this book and the lesson in which you can learn how to use each feature. You can also use the index to find specific information about a feature or about a task you want to perform. Appendix A, "Upgrading from FrontPage 98" details each new feature.

The New! 2000 icon appears in the margin throughout this book to indicate these new features of FrontPage 2000.

To learn how to	See
Manage a Web site with FrontPage.	Lesson 1
Create or edit a Web page with FrontPage's integrated Web page editor.	Lesson 2
Open recently used Webs in FrontPage.	Lesson 3
Use the FrontPage Themes dialog box to create an overall "look" for your Web.	Lesson 4
Change table properties.	Lesson 5
Use Cascading Style Sheets (CSS) to position items on Web pages.	Lesson 6
Test a form with FrontPage.	Lesson 7
Assign or create pages for Web site frames.	Lesson 8
Use background spelling checking.	Lesson 9
Animate text with dynamic HTML.	Lesson 10

Corrections, Comments, and Help

Every effort has been made to ensure the accuracy of this book and the contents of the FrontPage 2000 Step by Step CD-ROM. Microsoft Press provides corrections and additional content for its books through the World Wide Web at *mspress.microsoft.com/support*

If you have comments, questions, or ideas regarding this book or the CD-ROM, please send them to us.

Send e-mail to:

mspinput@microsoft.com

Or send postal mail to:

Microsoft Press

Attn: Step by Step Editor

One Microsoft Way

Redmond, WA 98052-6399

Please note that support for the FrontPage 2000 software product itself is not offered through the above addresses. For help using FrontPage 2000, you can call FrontPage 2000 Technical Support at (425) 635-7070 on weekdays between 6 A.M. and 6 P.M. Pacific Time.

Visit Our World Wide Web Site

We invite you to visit the Microsoft Press World Wide Web site. You can visit us at the following location:

mspress.microsoft.com

You'll find descriptions of all of our books, information about ordering titles, notices of special features and events, additional content for Microsoft Press books, and much more.

You can also find out the latest in software developments and news from Microsoft Corporation by visiting the following World Wide Web site:

microsoft.com

We look forward to your visit on the Web!

Using the Microsoft FrontPage 2000 Step by Step CD-ROM

The CD-ROM inside the back cover of this book contains the practice files that you'll use as you perform the exercises in the book and multimedia files that demonstrate ten of the exercises. By using the practice files, you won't waste time creating the samples used in the lessons, and you can concentrate on learning how to use Microsoft FrontPage 2000. With the files and the step by step instructions in the lessons, you'll also learn by doing, which is an easy and effective way to acquire and remember new skills.

important

Before you break the seal on the Microsoft FrontPage 2000 Step by Step CD-ROM package, be sure that this book matches your version of the software. This book is designed for use with Microsoft FrontPage 2000. If your product is not compatible with this book, a Step by Step book matching your software is probably available. Please visit our World Wide Web site at *mspress.microsoft.com* or call 1-800-MSPRESS (1-800-677-7377) for more information.

Installing the Practice Files

Follow these steps to install the practice files on your computer's hard disk so that you can use them with the exercises in this book.

1 If your computer isn't on, turn it on now.

2 If you're connected to a network, you will see a dialog box asking for your user name and password.

Close

3 Type your user name and password in the appropriate boxes, and click OK. If you see the Welcome dialog box, click the Close button.

4 Remove the CD-ROM from the package inside the back cover of this book.

5 Insert the CD-ROM in the CD-ROM drive of your computer. In My Computer, double-click your CD-ROM drive.

6 Double-click Setup, and then follow the instructions on the screen.

The setup program window appears with recommended options preselected for you. For best results in using the practice files with this book, accept these preselected settings.

7 When the files have been installed, remove the CD-ROM from your CD-ROM drive and replace it in the package inside the back cover of the book.

A folder called FrontPage 2000 SBS Practice has been created on your hard disk, and the practice files have been placed in that folder.

If your computer is set up to connect to the Internet, you can double-click the Microsoft Press Welcome shortcut to visit the Microsoft Press Web site. You can also connect to this Web site directly at *mspress.microsoft.com*.

Using the Practice Files

Each lesson in this book explains when and how to use any practice files for that lesson. The lessons are built around scenarios that simulate a real work environment, so you can easily apply the skills you learn to your own work. For the scenario in this book, imagine you are an executive in the small public relations firm, Impact Public Relations. The firm specializes in designing multimedia campaigns including print, radio, and television ads for mid-sized companies.

important

You do not have to work through the exercises in a lesson sequentially. However, before you can work through any subsequent exercises in any lesson, you must work through the exercise "Import the Lesson Web" in each lesson, which creates the practice Web for that lesson.

For those of you who like to know all the details, here's a list of the practice files used in the lessons. For the convenience of readers who don't want to work from the beginning of each lesson, separate practice files are included.

Filename	Description
Lesson01 - folder	Folder used in Lesson 1
Welcome.htm	File used in Lesson 1
Lesson02 - folder	Folder used in Lesson 2
Recreati.htm	File used in Lesson 2
Boat_trips.jpg	Picture used in Lesson 2
Pool01.jpg	Picture used in Lesson 2
Tennis_courts.jpg	Picture used in Lesson 2
Location02.htm	File used in Lesson 2
Extras - folder	Folder used in Lesson 2
Lesson03 - folder	Folder used in Lesson 3
Index.htm	File used in Lesson 3
Location.htm	File used in Lesson 3
Index01.htm	File used in Lesson 3
Index02.htm	File used in Lesson 3
FAQ.htm	File used in Lesson 3
Main_building.jpg	Picture used in Lesson 3
*Lesson04 - folder	Folder used in Lesson 4
Copyrigh.htm	File used in Lesson 4
Reasons.htm	File used in Lesson 4
Lesson05 - folder	Folder used in Lesson 5
Special_programs_for_kids01.htm	File used in Lesson 5
Directions_to_lakewood.htm	File used in Lesson 5
On_the_town01.htm	File used in Lesson 5
Exptextb.jpg	Picture used in Lesson 5
Lesson06 - folder	Folder used in Lesson 6
Welcome01.htm	File used in Lesson 6
Sights01.htm	File used in Lesson 6
Sights02.htm	File used in Lesson 6
Bry_gap.jpg	Picture used in Lesson 6
FP Logo.gif	Image used in Lesson 6
Welcome02.htm	File used in Lesson 6

Filename	Description
Welcome03.htm	File used in Lesson 6
Tolizt01.mid	Sound clip used in Lesson 6
Pc_help01.htm	File used in Lesson 6
Closewin.avi	Motion clip used in Lesson 6
Pc_help03.htm	File used in Lesson 6
Dragdrop.avi	Motion clip used in Lesson 6
Bry_gap_small.jpg	Picture used in Lesson 6
Shore_small.jpg	Picture used in Lesson 6
Frontdr01.htm	File used in Lesson 6
The Microsoft Sound.wav	Sound clip used in Lesson 6
Review02 - folder	Folder used in Review & Practice 2
Lesson07 - folder	Folder used in Lesson 7
Lesson08 - folder	Folder used in Lesson 8
Menu01.htm	File used in Lesson 8
Roomres.htm	File used in Lesson 8
Location1.htm	File used in Lesson 8
Frontdr.htm	File used in Lesson 8
Index03.htm	File used in Lesson 8
Location.htm	File used in Lesson 8
Onthe.htm	File used in Lesson 8
Review03 - folder	Folder used in Review & Practice 3
Lesson09 - folder	Folder used in Lesson 9
History.htm	File used in Lesson 9
Dining.htm	File used in Lesson 9
Lesson10 - folder	Folder used in Lesson 10
Dhtml01.htm	File used in Lesson 10
Review04 - folder	Folder used in Lesson 10
Coffeeshop_sign.jpg	Picture used in Lesson 10
Menu.htm	File used in Lesson 10

* There is not a Review01 folder because there are no exercise files for the Part 1 Review & Practice.

Using the Multimedia Files

Throughout this book, you will see icons for movie files for particular exercises. Use the following steps to play the multimedia files.

① Insert the Microsoft FrontPage 2000 Step by Step CD-ROM in your CD-ROM drive.

② On the Windows taskbar, click the Start button, point to Programs, and then click Windows Explorer.

③ In the All Folders area, click the drive D icon (or the appropriate CD-ROM drive letter).

The contents of the CD-ROM are displayed.

④ In the Contents Of area, double-click the Multimedia folder.

The Multimedia folder opens.

⑤ Double-click the multimedia file that you want to view.

Windows Media Player runs the video of the exercise.

Close

⑥ After the video is finished, click the Close button in the top-right corner of the Media Player window.

Media Player closes and you return to Windows Explorer.

⑦ Close Windows Explorer, and return to the exercise in the book.

Replying to Install Messages

You might see a message indicating that the feature you are trying to use is not installed. If you see this message, insert your FrontPage 2000 CD or Microsoft Office 2000 CD 1 in your CD-ROM drive, and click Yes to install the feature.

Uninstalling the Practice Files

Use the following steps when you want to delete the practice files added to your hard disk by the Step by Step setup program.

① On the Windows taskbar, click the Start button, point to Settings, and then click Control Panel.

② Double-click the Add/Remove icon.

The Add/Remove Programs Properties dialog box appears.

③ Click Microsoft FrontPage 2000 Step by Step Practice from the list, and then click Add/Remove.

A confirmation message is displayed.

④ Click Yes.

The practice files are uninstalled.

⑤ Click OK to close the Add/Remove Programs Properties dialog box.

⑥ Close the Control Panel window.

Need Help with the Practice Files?

Every effort has been made to ensure the accuracy of this book and the contents of the CD-ROM. If you do run into a problem, Microsoft Press provides corrections for its books through the World Wide Web at:

mspress.microsoft.com/support/

We invite you to visit our main Web page at:

mspress.microsoft.com

You'll find descriptions for all of our books, information about ordering titles, notices of special features and events, additional content for Microsoft Press books, and much more.

Conventions and Features in This Book

You can save time when you use this book by understanding, before you start the lessons, how instructions, keys to press, and so on are shown in the book. Please take a moment to read the following list, which also points out helpful features of the book that you might want to use.

Conventions

- Hands-on exercises for you to follow are given in numbered lists of steps (1, 2, and so on). A round bullet (●) indicates an exercise that has only one step.

- Text that you are to type appears in **bold**.

- A plus sign (+) between two key names means that you must press those keys at the same time. For example, "Press Alt+Tab" means that you hold down the Alt key while you press Tab.

- The icons on the following page are used to identify certain types of exercise features:

Icon	Alerts you to
	Skills that are demonstrated in audiovisual files available on the Microsoft FrontPage 2000 Step by Step CD-ROM.
	New features in FrontPage 2000.

Other Features of This Book

■ You can get a quick reminder of how to perform the tasks you learned by reading the Quick Reference at the end of a lesson.

■ You can practice the major skills presented in the lessons by working through the Review & Practice section at the end of each part.

■ You can see a multimedia demonstration of some of the exercises in the book by following the instructions in the "Using the Multimedia Files" exercise in the "Using the Microsoft FrontPage 2000 Step by Step CD-ROM" section of this book.

PART 1

Planning and Creating a Web Site

1

Planning a Web Site

ESTIMATED TIME 20 min.

In this lesson you will learn how to:

✔ *Plan a Web site.*

✔ *Start FrontPage.*

✔ *View a Web site in different ways.*

✔ *Open and close a Web.*

Imagine that you are an account executive at Impact Public Relations, an innovative public relations firm that uses the Internet to spread the word about its clients. You've just been assigned to an important new account with Lakewood Mountains Resort, a posh California vacation spot. Your first job will be to create a Web site that spotlights the resort's most attractive features.

There's just one problem. You've been on the World Wide Web, but you don't understand how it works. And the idea of *creating* a Web site—especially for a crucial new account—is very intimidating. But you're in luck. A fellow account executive tells you about a Web tool called Microsoft FrontPage 2000, and volunteers to help you along as you learn to use it.

In this lesson, you will learn how the Web operates and how Web pages make up Webs, or Web sites. You will also learn how to plan your own Web site, complete with hyperlinks. Finally, you will learn how to start FrontPage, use FrontPage views, open and close a Web, and quit FrontPage.

Understanding the World Wide Web

The World Wide Web (or the *Web*) makes it easy to use the *Internet*, a world-wide network of computers created in the late 1960s. Originally, the Internet required you to learn many arcane commands—not only to use it, but also to get data from computers connected to it. If you wanted to get data from a computer that used the UNIX operating system, for example, you needed to know the commands for using UNIX; to get data from a VAX computer that used the VMS operating system, you needed to know the commands for VMS. The Internet worked, but it was difficult to use.

In 1992, however, Tim Berners-Lee and other researchers helped launch the Web, which allowed users to "browse" the Internet without knowing complex commands. In the years that followed, Web *browsers* such as Microsoft Internet Explorer made the Web even easier and more powerful.

important

In this book (and elsewhere), you'll see the word *Web* used in two different ways. Usually, *Web* refers to the World Wide Web. However, it can also refer to a *FrontPage-based Web*, a set of Web pages you create in FrontPage for your Web site. The context should make it clear what *Web* means in each particular case.

The key to creating the Web was *hypertext,* a method for linking blocks, or "pages," of data that was first conceived in the 1960s. It wasn't until the 1990s, however, that Berners-Lee and his coworkers applied the hypertext concept to the Internet with what they called *HTTP* (Hypertext Transfer Protocol). And with HTTP, the World Wide Web was born.

Today, there are millions of Web sites. You can access information on a wide range of topics, you can run a Web-based business and you can even learn about the Web and its underlying technology.

Understanding Web Pages and HTML

If hypertext and HTTP were the keys to creating the World Wide Web, the key to creating Web pages is *HTML* (Hypertext Markup Language). *HTML* uses codes, called *tags*, to format and define text on a Web page. The Web browser that you use translates these codes into the Web page text and graphics you see on your screen.

HTML tags do more than tell Web browsers how to format text and place graphics. Hyperlinks, for example, tell the Web browser to locate a different

Web page on the Internet and display it on the user's screen. The code for a typical Web page and the page it creates are shown in the following illustrations.

Start of HTML document

Start of page header

End of page header

Start of table

Start of row in table

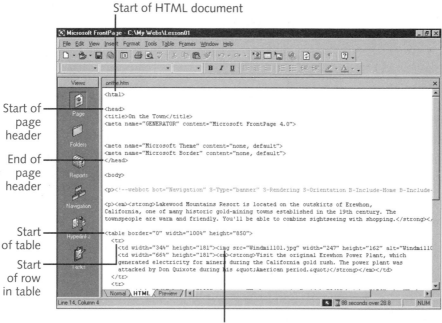

Image file inserted in table cell

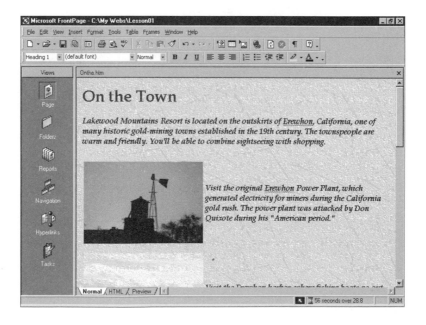

Many Web pages today use *scripts* created with languages such as Microsoft VBScript and JavaScript. These "mini-programs" are embedded in Web pages, where they handle formatting, images, and multimedia display routines much like any other programming language. A new and more advanced way to handle many scripting tasks is to use *Dynamic HTML* (DHTML). With DHTML, you can create simple animations and many other effects.

So, you're feeling overwhelmed by HTML and its many options? Now your coworker gives you the good news. To create Web sites with FrontPage, you don't have to learn anything about HTML, scripts, or DHTML unless you want to. With FrontPage, you simply type the text you want on your Web page, drop in any pictures or sounds you desire, and use FrontPage's features to do anything for which you would normally have to write a script or DHTML. You can still write HTML, scripts, or DHTML if you want, but it's not required.

tip
This book teaches you how to create Web sites for the World Wide Web. You can use the same techniques to create Web sites for an *intranet*—a network that works like the World Wide Web but has security features that restrict parts of it so that only users within your company or organization can access its pages.

Understanding Web Pages and Web Sites

You'll learn more about wizards and templates in Lesson 2, "Creating a Web Site."

A Web *site* is a collection of related Web pages and other files linked together. Web sites usually have a specific purpose, whether it be personal or business-related. FrontPage comes with *wizards*, which walk you step by step through the process of creating a Web site, and *templates*, which are built-in Web pages containing all the formatting required to build and customize your own Web pages. Wizards and templates can help you create several different kinds of Web sites.

A hyperlink is text or an image on a Web page that, when clicked, immediately sends you to another Web page or site.

On each Web site, one page is designated as the *home page*. This is the page that users see first when they visit the Web site. From the home page, users can click *hyperlinks* to jump to other pages on the Web site or to pages on different Web sites. Those hyperlinks might be Web sites on the same computer as the first Web site, or they might be stored on a computer halfway around the world. A typical Web site organization is shown in the following illustration.

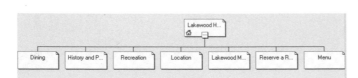

The home page is at the top, with linked pages on the row below it. Usually, each page under the home page—called a "child page" of the home page— contains hyperlinks to the other pages on the Web site, as well as hyperlinks back to the home page. Often, child pages will have hyperlinks to still other pages that are below them in the organization, and so forth.

You can use FrontPage to create and manage Web sites on the Internet or on an intranet.

A Web site resides on a *Web server,* which is a computer dedicated to making Web pages available to people who want to visit the site. (However, with FrontPage, you can create your Web site right in your computer's file system and publish the Web site to a server when you are ready.) Normally, a Web server is connected to the Internet, which makes its Web pages available for viewing on the World Wide Web. Many companies and organizations are setting up Web servers on intranets. These private Web servers are ideal for hosting Web sites that contain project files and other internal data that need to be shared by staff members. Some pages of the intranet Web site are made available to the world, while other pages remain accessible only to users within the organization.

Finding a Web Server

Before you set up the Web site for your client, Lakewood Mountains Resort, you need to find a place to put it: a Web server.

Most Internet service providers (ISPs) offer Web hosting as part of the package when you buy an Internet account. Web hosting simply means that the ISP provides space on a Web server computer for your Web files. Online services such as America Online also offer Web hosting. For simple Webs, an ISP's Web hosting services are often adequate. For larger and more sophisticated Webs, though, an account with a *dedicated* Web host can be a good investment. A dedicated Web host can offer more disk space for your Web files and, often, faster equipment.

Whether you choose an Internet service provider or a dedicated Web host, there's an important question you should always ask: "Do you have the FrontPage Server Extensions?" FrontPage has a slew of extra features to help you create exciting Web sites and put them on the Web with minimal effort. But some ISPs and Web hosts do not have the FrontPage Server Extensions. Some ISPs have them for business Internet accounts but not for the less-expensive personal accounts.

So, where can you find a FrontPage-supporting Web host? On the Web, of course. Navigate to Microsoft's Web Presence Provider site at *microsoft.saltmine.com/frontpage/wpp/list/* to view lists of ISPs and Web hosts that have the FrontPage Server Extensions.

Planning a Web Site

Planning Your Web Site

Let's assume you've found a Web host that has the FrontPage Server Extensions. Now you need to decide what should go into the Web site you present to your client. You must first decide on the purpose of the Web site. In the case of Lakewood Mountains Resort, there are two main purposes.

- To provide information about the resort for prospective customers.
- To enable customers to request room reservations over the Web.

Of course, Web sites can have many additional purposes. One Web site might provide technical support for a computer product. Another might have a catalog and allow customers to place secure orders over the Web. The purpose of a Web site determines its design and the pages it should include.

Like all Web sites, the resort's Web site will start with a home page. From there, it needs at least one page about each of the resort's major selling points. So that customers can request reservations over the Web, the site will also need a form on which customers can enter their name, address, and reservation data.

You call the resort manager to learn about the resort's major selling points. You end up with a list of topics, each of which will get its own Web page.

- The resort's secluded location.
- The resort's recreational facilities.
- The resort's fine food.
- The picturesque town just a few minutes away.
- The resort's colorful history and helpful staff.

Based on this information, you come up with a diagram of the Web site.

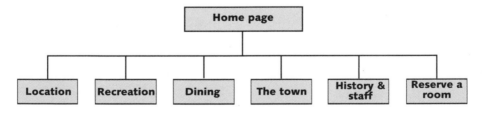

Now is the time to ask how the pages will be linked together. The obvious answer is "by hyperlinks," but FrontPage helps you use hyperlinks in a variety of ways. You can put all your hyperlinks on the home page, or, if you're interested in a more high-tech alternative, you can use a *navigation bar*, one of FrontPage's special features. You can also create an *image map*—a picture with "hot spots," or hyperlinks within an image, that users can click to go to the desired pages.

Your coworker suggests a simple yet elegant solution: a menu *frame*. A frame is a pane in a Web site that works independently of the main pane. A frame is displayed continuously even as the user selects other hyperlinks that are displayed in the main pane. As the user moves around the Web site, pages are displayed in the right frame, while a menu of hyperlinks stays constant in the left frame. After considering these options, you decide to use frames in the Web site.

Managing a Web Site with FrontPage

FrontPage makes it easy not only to create Web pages and Web sites, but also to manage them. The FrontPage window is divided into three main sections, each of which gives you a different kind of control over your Web site.

New!
2000

The Views bar now provides an easy way to switch between views of Web structure and pages, and it includes an all new Reports view.

Views bar   Folder List   Page view

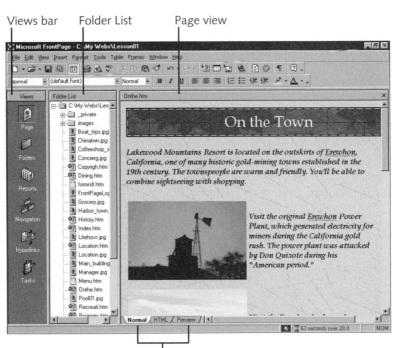

Tabs let you view and edit the currently selected file in different ways.

In FrontPage, you can view a Web in several different ways. The Views bar displays icons that let you view and edit different aspects of your Web.

Icon	Name	Description
	Folders	Displays a list of folders and files in the current Web.
	Reports	Displays a list of reports on different aspects of the current Web, such as the number of linked files, broken links, and the number of "slow" pages that would take more than 30 seconds to download to a computer over a 28.8-KB connection. (Thirty seconds is the default value, but it can be changed by the user.)
	Navigation	Displays a tree diagram of the current Web and makes the Folder List display a list of folders and files in the current Web.
	Tasks	Displays a list of tasks to be done on the current Web. When you use some of the wizards to create a Web, FrontPage compiles a task list. You can also add tasks on your own.
	Page	Displays a Web page for viewing or editing.
	Hyperlinks	Displays a diagram of hyperlinks to and from the current page.

You'll learn more about tasks in Lesson 10, "Managing and Enhancing a Web."

The Folder List displays all folders and files in the current Web, while the currently selected page is displayed in Page view. At the bottom of the screen, a status bar displays information about the current page or operation. When a page is displayed in Page view, for example, the status bar shows an estimated download time for the page over a 28.8-KB modem connection.

Before you can work with any of the exercise files, you must install the files from the Microsoft FrontPage 2000 Step by Step CD-ROM. For installation instructions, see "Installing the Practice Files" on page xviii.

Import the Lesson 1 practice Web

In this exercise, you create a new Web based on the files in the Lesson01 folder in the FrontPage 2000 SBS Practice folder. You will use this Web for all the exercises in Lesson 1.

1 On the Windows taskbar, click the Start button, point to Programs, and then click Microsoft FrontPage.

FrontPage starts.

If a dialog box appears asking if you'd like to make FrontPage your default HTML editor, click Yes.

② On the File menu, point to New, and then click Web.

FrontPage displays the New dialog box.

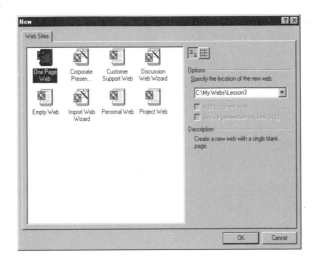

If your hard disk drive is not drive C, substitute the appropriate drive letter in step 3.

FrontPage will create the Lesson01 directory for you.

③ Click the Import Web Wizard icon. In the Specify The Location Of The New Web text box, delete the default text and type **C:\My Webs\Lesson01**, and then click OK.

FrontPage displays the first Import Web Wizard dialog box.

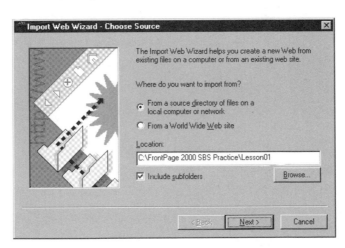

④ Click the From A Source Directory Of Files option, click the Include Subfolders check box, and click the Browse button.

⑤ Browse to the Lesson01 folder in the FrontPage 2000 SBS Practice folder, and click OK.

6 Click Next twice, and then click Finish.

FrontPage creates a new Web based on the practice files and places it in the Lesson01 folder.

Explore FrontPage views

In this exercise, you explore different views of your new Web.

In the Folder List, an icon appears next to each filename, indicating the type of file (Web page, image file, and so forth).

1 If your Web is not already displayed in Page view, on the Views bar, click the Page icon.

2 In the Folder List, double-click the file Welcome.htm.

FrontPage displays the Welcome Web page.

On the status bar, FrontPage estimates the amount of time the current page will take to download over a 28.8-KB modem connection.

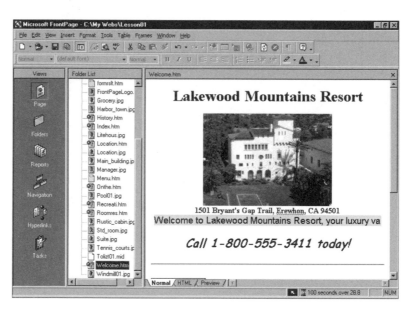

For a demonstration of how to explore FrontPage views, in the Multimedia folder on the Microsoft FrontPage 2000 Step by Step CD-ROM, double-click the FrontPage Views icon.

3 At the bottom of the FrontPage window, click the HTML tab.

FrontPage displays the HTML code for the current page.

4 At the bottom of the FrontPage window, click the Preview tab.

FrontPage displays a preview of how the page will look in a Web browser.

5 On the Views bar, click the Folders icon.

FrontPage displays a list of all folders and files in the current Web.

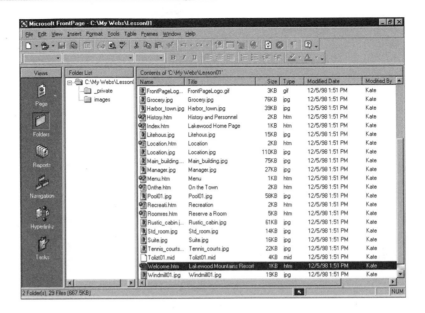

6   On the Views bar, click the Reports icon.

FrontPage displays a list of reports about the current Web.

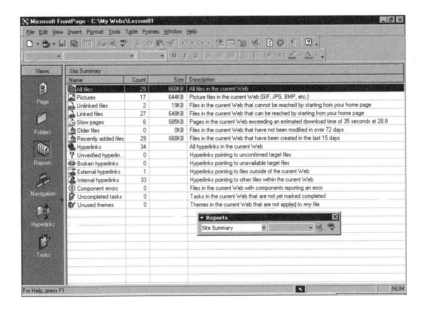

You can use the Reports toolbar to switch quickly between different report views.

In the Navigation view's tree diagram, you can drag Web pages to restructure your Web.

7   On the Views bar, click the Navigation icon.

FrontPage normally displays a tree diagram of the current Web. However, because you haven't yet created any Web pages, there is no tree diagram to display.

8   On the Views bar, click the Hyperlinks icon.

FrontPage displays a diagram of hyperlinks going to and from the page.

9   On the Views bar, click the Tasks icon.

Currently, there are no tasks to display.

Understanding FrontPage Folders

When you install FrontPage 2000, it creates a folder called "My Webs."
This is the default folder in which FrontPage will store any Webs you
create. Each separate Web you create gets its own subfolder in the My
Webs folder in which FrontPage stores files specific to that Web.

When FrontPage creates a Web, it also creates at least three different folders in which to store Web pages and files. You don't have to worry about
these folders: you can ignore them and your Web will still work perfectly.
However, understanding these folders gives you insight into your Web and
can help you organize your files.

Folder	Explanation
Main folder	Default folder for your Web page, image, and Java class files.
_private	FrontPage stores files used to organize and manage your Web in this folder. Should be left strictly alone.
Images	Folder into which you can move image files if desired. If you have a large number of image files, this helps remove clutter from your main folder.

(continued)

continued

In addition to the three default folders, you can also create your own folders to hold specific types or groups of files.

Create a folder

❶   On the Views bar, click the Folders icon.

❷   On the File menu, point to New, and then click Folder.

FrontPage creates a new folder. The default folder name is New Folder.

❸   Delete the default folder name, type the desired name, and press Enter.

FrontPage renames the folder.

You can create a new folder for any purpose. The only thing you must remember is to use FrontPage—not the Windows Explorer—to move files into the folder. When you use FrontPage to move files, any hyperlinks to those files are automatically updated.

Close and reopen a Web

In this exercise, you close and reopen the Lesson01 Web.

❶   On the File menu, click Close Web.

FrontPage closes the Lesson01 Web.

❷   On the File menu, click Open Web.

FrontPage displays the Open Web dialog box.

❸ If necessary, browse to the Lesson01 Web in the My Webs folder.

❹ If necessary, in the file list, click the Lesson01 folder.

❺ Click the Open button.

FrontPage opens the Web.

❻ On the Views bar, click the Page icon, and then in the Folder List, double-click the file History.htm.

FrontPage displays the History and Personnel Web page.

One Step Further Getting Ideas for a Web Site

You've tentatively decided to use frames in your Web for Lakewood Mountains Resort, but you'd like to get some more ideas for enhancing your Web. Your coworker suggests that the best place to look is the Web itself.

The first and most obvious place to look is Microsoft's own FrontPage Web site at *www.microsoft.com/frontpage*. Another place to look is CNet's Builder.com Web site at *www.builder.com*. This site has tutorials on Web design, HTML, scripting, and many other Web topics.

Finally, you should surf the Web to view as many Web pages as you can. Ideas are everywhere, and as long as you don't just copy the content of someone's Web site, the ideas are free. You'll often find some of the most innovative and appealing Web ideas at some of the most unusual—even bizarre—Web sites.

Get ideas for your Web site

In this exercise, you visit Web pages on the Internet to familiarize yourself with some of the places that offer ideas on Web design.

❶ Connect to the Internet, and then double-click the Web browser icon on the Windows desktop.

Your Web browser opens and displays your Internet home page.

❷ In the Address bar, type **microsoft.com/clipgallerylive**, and press Enter.

The End User License Agreement (EULA) is displayed.

❸ Read the license agreement, and then click the Accept button.

The Microsoft Clip Gallery Live Web page is displayed in your browser. From here you can download clip art, photo images, sounds, and videos.

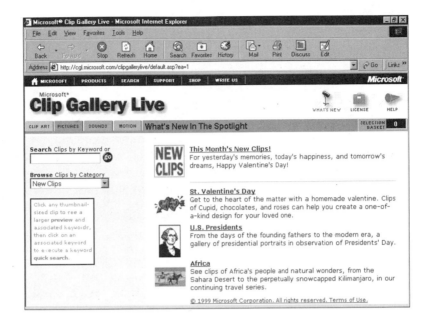

Microsoft's Clip Gallery Live page is continuously updated. If you visit the page on the Web, it will look different from the figure shown here.

4 In the Address bar, type **microsoft.com/frontpage**

Microsoft's FrontPage Web site is displayed in your browser.

5 In the Address bar, type **www.builder.com**, and then press Enter.

The CNet Builder.com Web page is displayed in your browser.

Finish the lesson

Close

1 Click the Close button at the top-right corner of your Web browser window.

Your Web browser closes and FrontPage reappears.

2 On the File menu, click Close Web.

3 For each page, if FrontPage prompts you to save changes, click Yes.

FrontPage saves your changes and closes the Lesson01 Web.

Lesson 1 Quick Reference

To	Do this	Icon
Plan a Web site	Decide on the purposes of the Web site, and then decide what Web pages are needed for the site.	
Start FrontPage	Click the Start button, point to Programs, and click Microsoft FrontPage.	
Create a new Web based on Web page files in a folder	On the File menu, point to New, and click Web. In the New dialog box, click the Import Web Wizard icon. In the Specify The Location Of The New Web text box, type the folder containing the files for the new Web. Click OK, click the From A Source Directory Of Files option, click the Include Subfolders check box, and click the Browse button. Browse to the folder that you want to import, click OK, click Next twice, and then click Finish.	
Open a Web	On the File menu, click Open Web. In the Open Web dialog box, browse to the folder containing the Web, and click the Open button.	
View or edit a Web page	Double-click the filename (with an .htm extension) in the Folder List.	
Preview the appearance of a Web page in Page view	Click the Page icon on the Views bar, and click the Preview tab at the bottom of the FrontPage window.	
View a tree diagram of a Web structure	Click the Navigation icon on the Views bar.	
View a diagram of hyperlinks to and from a Web page	Click the Web page filename in the Folder List, and then click the Hyperlinks icon on the Views bar.	
View a list of tasks required to complete a Web site	Click the Tasks icon on the Views bar.	
View a list of folders and files in a Web	Click the Folders icon on the Views bar.	
View reports about a Web	Click the Reports icon on the Views bar.	

2

Creating a Web Site

**ESTIMATED
TIME
40 min.**

In this lesson you will learn how to:

✔ *Create a Web.*

✔ *Create a home page.*

✔ *Add and format Web page text.*

✔ *Add a scrolling marquee to a Web page.*

✔ *Preview a Web.*

✔ *Add pages to a Web.*

✔ *Change Web page properties.*

✔ *Organize a Web.*

Now that you've defined the purposes of the Lakewood Mountains Resort Web site and determined which pages it should include, it's time to start creating the Web site in Microsoft FrontPage 2000. That's the good news. But your boss just stuck his head in your office and announced that you're meeting with the client tomorrow afternoon. A first draft of the Web site has to be ready for presentation at the meeting.

In this lesson, you will learn about FrontPage tools that can help you create a Web site in record time. You will then create a Web and add a home page. You will enter and format text on the page, add a scrolling marquee, create another page, and import an existing page. You will change the properties of a Web page and preview your Web. Finally, you will learn how to organize your Web.

Creating a Web Site Using a Wizard

There are three ways to create a Web in FrontPage: use a wizard, use a template, or create the Web "from scratch." The method you choose depends on your specific needs and situation.

FrontPage wizards are best used for complex Web sites. Each wizard creates a different type of Web using a series of dialog boxes in which you select the specific options that fit your situation.

When you've made all your selections, the wizard creates the Web site based on your input. FrontPage includes the wizards described in the following sections.

Corporate Presence Wizard

The Corporate Presence Wizard creates a Web site for a company. The Web site includes a home page, a table of contents, a News Release page, a product and service directory, a Web page for each product or service, a Customer Feedback page, and a Web page that lets visitors search your site.

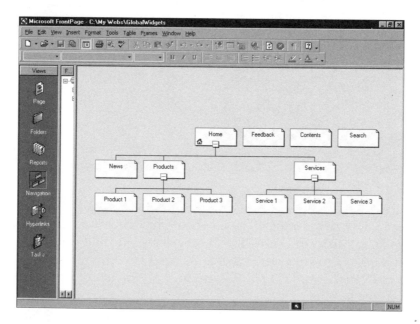

Discussion Web Wizard

The Discussion Web Wizard creates a Web site with a threaded message board, which allows visitors to view, post, and reply to messages on your Web site.

Import Web Wizard

The Import Web Wizard creates a new Web site based on existing Web files on your own computer or on a Web server. You can then modify the Web pages and Web structure as needed. You'll find this wizard especially useful for creating and testing updated versions of your own Web sites.

Create a Web site using a Wizard

In this exercise, you create a Web site using the Corporate Presence Wizard.

❶ On the File menu, point to New, and then click Web.

FrontPage displays the New dialog box.

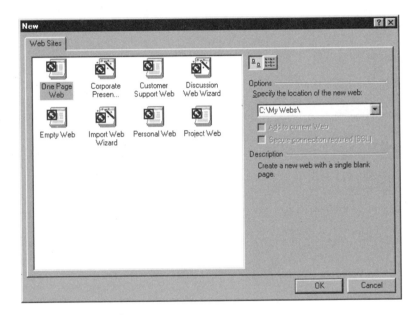

❷ In the Web Sites pane, click the Corporate Presence icon.

FrontPage will use the Corporate Presence Wizard to create the Web.

If your hard disk drive is not drive C, substitute the appropriate drive letter in step 3.

❸ In the Specify The Location Of The New Web text box, delete the default text and type **C:\My Webs\MyWizardDemo**.

FrontPage will create the C:\My Webs\MyWizardDemo folder. It will put all the Web files in that folder and its subfolders.

❹ Click OK, and then click Next.

FrontPage displays the first Corporate Presence Web Wizard dialog box, which explains the purpose of the Wizard. It then displays the second dialog box, in which you can select pages to include in the Web.

The Corporate Web Wizard displays different dialog boxes depending on which pages you select for inclusion in your corporate Web.

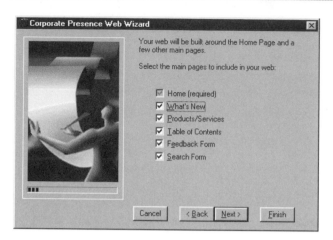

5   Click the What's New check box and the Search Form check box to clear them, and then click Next.

FrontPage will not include a What's New or a Search Form page in the Web. FrontPage displays the next dialog box, in which you select the information to be displayed on your corporate home page.

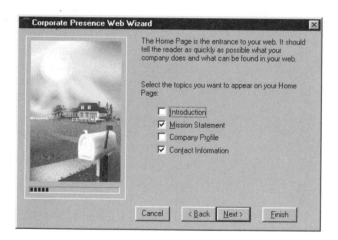

6   Click the Introduction check box to select it, and then click Next.

FrontPage will display an introduction on your corporate home page. FrontPage displays the next dialog box, in which you select how many pages the wizard should create to show information about products and services.

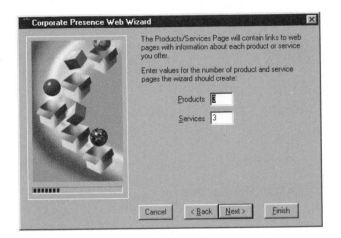

7 Click Next.

FrontPage accepts the default settings of three Product pages and three Services pages and displays a dialog box in which you can select the information you want displayed on each product or service Web page.

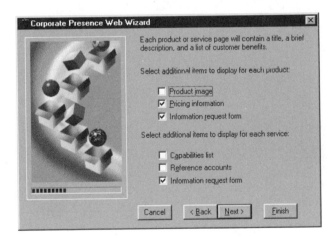

8 Click Next.

FrontPage accepts the default settings and displays a dialog box in which you can select the information you want to collect from Web site visitors who respond on your Feedback page.

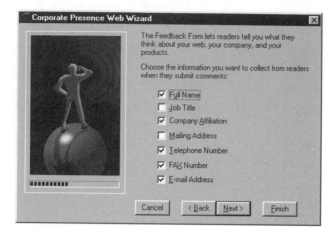

9 Click Next five times.

FrontPage displays a dialog box in which you enter the name and address of your company.

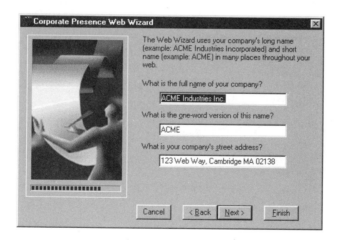

To keep this exercise brief, you skipped several dialog boxes you would normally complete, such as one in which you enter your company's phone number.

10 In the What Is The Full Name Of Your Company text box, type **Lakewood Mountains Resort**. Press Tab, type **Lakewood**, press Tab, type **1501 Bryant's Gap Trail, Erewhon, CA 94501**, and click Finish.

FrontPage creates a corporate presence Web based on the options you selected and the information you entered.

11 On the Views bar, click the Navigation icon, and in Navigation view, double-click the Home page icon.

FrontPage displays your corporate home page. You can now modify the page by entering additional information.

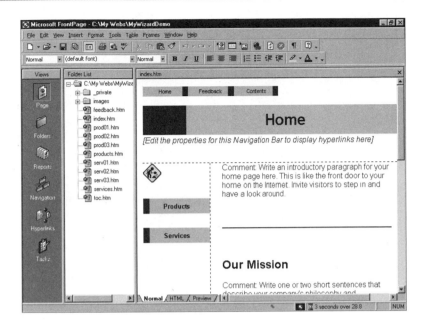

⑫ On the File menu, click Close Web.

FrontPage closes the Corporate Presence Web you just created.

tip

When you are creating Web filenames, get into the habit of creating names that do not contain spaces. Most Web servers do not recognize spaces in filenames. If you want to keep your Web filenames descriptive, you can separate words and still keep them connected by placing the underscore character (_) between words.

Corporate Presence Web Pages

The Corporate Presence Wizard can include several ready-to-use pages on your Web site. Even if you don't use the Corporate Presence Wizard, you can create these pages individually by using Web page templates. To use a template to create a page, click the Page icon on the Views bar. On the File menu, point to New, and click Page. FrontPage displays the New dialog box with a menu of page templates. Click the icon for the type of page you want to create, and then click OK.

(continued)

continued

Page template	Creates
Home	A home page containing information you specify.
What's New	A page with information about new pages or other updates on the Web site.
Products/Services	One or more pages about products or services offered by your company, with a description of each product or service, benefits, part numbers, and pricing.
Table of Contents	Lists all the pages in the Web site, with a hyperlink to each page.
Feedback Form	Allows Web site visitors to send feedback to an e-mail address you specify.
Search Form	Allows Web site visitors to search the Web site for pages containing words they specify.

Creating a Web Site Using a Template

Unlike wizards, which prompt you for input and then design a Web based on that input, templates are ready-made Web sites that you can modify for your own needs. FrontPage includes the following templates.

This template	Creates
Customer Support Web	A Web site in which a company can answer customer questions and get feedback. It combines a message board with several other features, such as a frequently asked questions list (FAQ), a suggestion form, and an area for downloading information and software.
Project Web	A Web site to share information about a project with members of the project team. It includes a page that lists team members, a schedule page, a project status page, a message board, and a search page.
Personal Web	A Web site to showcase the interests of an individual. It includes a home page, a photo album page, an interests page, and a Web page for links to other Web sites.
One Page Web	A Web site with only a home page.
Empty Web	A Web site that you build from scratch. It does not include any Web pages.

Create a Web site using a template

In this exercise, you create a Web using the Customer Support Web template.

If you completed the previous exercise, notice that FrontPage has suggested MyWizardDemo2 as the name of your new Web because the last Web you created was named MyWizardDemo.

❶ On the File menu, point to New, and then click Web.

FrontPage displays the New dialog box.

❷ In the Web sites pane, click the Customer Support Web icon.

FrontPage will use the Customer Support Web template. This creates a Web site designed to provide help and solve problems for users of a company's products.

❸ In the Specify The Location Of The New Web text box, delete the default text and type **C:\My Webs\MyTempDemo**, and click OK.

FrontPage creates a new Web based on the Customer Support template.

If your hard disk drive is not drive C, substitute the appropriate drive letter in step 3.

❹ In the Folder List, double-click the file Index.htm.

FrontPage displays the new Web's home page.

Unlike a wizard, which asks you a series of questions about your Web, a template is a blueprint used to create a particular kind of Web. Once you've created the Web, you can then modify it to suit your needs.

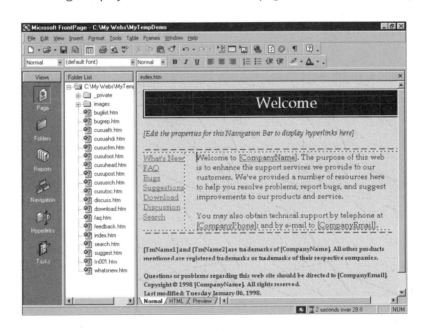

❺ On the displayed Web page, select the text *[CompanyName]*, and then type **Lakewood Mountains Software**.

FrontPage replaces the selected text with the text you typed.

❻ On the toolbar, click the Save button.

FrontPage saves the Web page with your changes.

Save

7 In the Folder List, double-click the file Bugrep.htm.

FrontPage displays the Web page that allows users to report problems in the company's products or services.

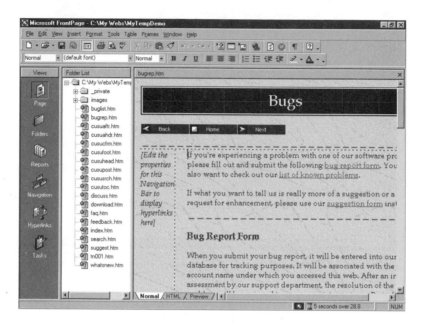

8 In the Folder List, double-click the file Discuss.htm.

FrontPage displays the Web page that allows users to read and respond to messages in a discussion board.

9 On the File menu, click Close Web.

FrontPage closes the Web you just created.

Creating and Importing Webs

Whether you use wizards or templates, there are essentially two ways to create a Web. The first way is to create the Web's pages and other files after you create the Web itself. The second way is to create a new Web based on existing files.

The second approach works especially well when you have a previous version of a Web—whether on your local hard disk drive or on a remote Web server—and you want to create a new version of the Web.

Create an empty Web

In this exercise, you create a new Web using the Empty Web template. You then close the empty Web.

1 On the File menu, point to New, and then click Web.

FrontPage displays the New dialog box.

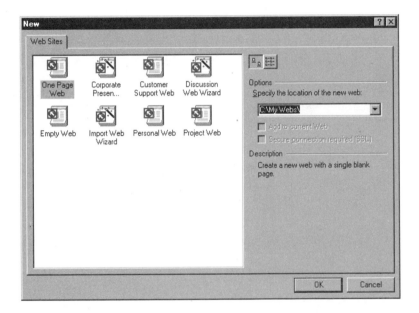

If your hard disk drive is not drive C, substitute the appropriate drive letter in step 2.

2 Click the Empty Web icon. In the Specify The Location Of The New Web text box, delete the default text and type **C:\My Webs\Empty02**, and then click OK.

FrontPage creates a folder named Empty02 and places a new, empty Web in the folder.

3 On the Views bar, click the Navigation icon.

FrontPage normally displays a tree diagram of the current Web. However, because you haven't yet created any Web pages, there is no tree diagram to display.

4 On the File menu, click Close Web.

FrontPage closes the empty Web.

Import the Lesson 2 practice Web

In this exercise, you create a new Web based on the files in the Lesson02 folder in the FrontPage 2000 SBS Practice folder. You will use this Web for all the remaining exercises in Lesson 2.

1 On the File menu, point to New, and then click Web.

FrontPage displays the New dialog box.

If your hard disk drive is not drive C, substitute the appropriate drive letter in step 2.

2 Click the Import Web Wizard icon. In the Specify The Location Of The New Web text box, type **C:\My Webs\Lesson02**, and then click OK.

FrontPage displays the first Import Web Wizard dialog box.

3 Click the From A Source Directory Of Files option, click the Include Subfolders check box, and click the Browse button.

4 Browse to the Lesson 02 folder in the FrontPage 2000 SBS Practice folder, and click OK.

5 Click Next twice, and then click Finish.

FrontPage creates a new Web based on the practice files and places it in the Lesson02 folder.

Creating a Home Page and Adding Text

Once you've created a Web, the next step is to add Web pages. By default, the first page you add will be treated as your Web's home page. The filename for the home page is either Default.htm or Index.htm, although the Web page title can be anything you choose.

tip
Web servers don't all use the same conventions for naming home pages. Most require this file to be named either Default.htm or Index.htm. If your home page name is different from what the Web server you're publishing to requires, don't worry; FrontPage automatically renames the home page when you publish a Web to a server. (If you're uploading files manually instead of having FrontPage publish them for you—as you must with popular Web sites such as GeoCities or The Globe—you will have to rename the file yourself.)

FrontPage makes it easy to add text and other elements to Web pages. To add text, you simply type it on the page. You can then apply standard Web text styles to the text. You can also format text (and other Web page elements) with FrontPage's own formatting tools and styles for headings or body text. There's even a Formatting toolbar with the same buttons as those in Microsoft Word and other familiar Microsoft Office programs.

Create and title a Web page

If you are not working through this lesson sequentially, follow the steps in "Import the Lesson 2 Practice Web" earlier in this lesson.

In this exercise, you create a home page for Lakewood Mountains Resort.

① On the Views bar, click the Navigation icon.

② On the File menu, point to New, and then click Page.

FrontPage creates a new Web page and displays it as an icon.

New button

You can also click the New button on the toolbar to create a new page.

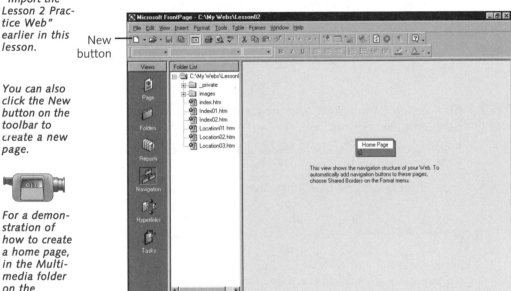

For a demonstration of how to create a home page, in the Multimedia folder on the Microsoft FrontPage 2000 Step by Step CD-ROM, double-click the HomePage icon.

③ In the home page icon, click the text *Home Page* to select it, type **Lakewood Mountains Resort**, and then press Enter.

FrontPage retitles the Web page.

Add and format text

In this exercise, you open the Lakewood Mountains Resort home page for editing. You then add and format text on the page.

1 Make sure your Web is displayed in Navigation view. Double-click the Lakewood Mountains Resort home page icon.

FrontPage displays the home page in Page view.

2 Type **Lakewood Mountains Resort** (but do not press Enter).

3 The Text Style box at the left end of the Formatting toolbar currently says Normal. Click the drop-down arrow to expand the list.

The Text Style list shows available text styles.

Center

4 Click Heading 1 in the list, and then on the Formatting toolbar, click the Center button.

FrontPage formats the line in Heading 1 style and centers the heading horizontally on the Web page.

5 Press Enter twice, and type **1501 Bryant's Gap Trail, Erewhon, CA 94501**

tip

Notice that FrontPage underlines the word *Erewhon*. This indicates that the FrontPage spelling checker did not find the word in its word list and that it might be misspelled. However, you know that it is the proper name of a town and is spelled correctly. You'll learn how to use FrontPage's spelling checker in Lesson 9; just ignore the underlining for now.

6 Select the text in the address line.

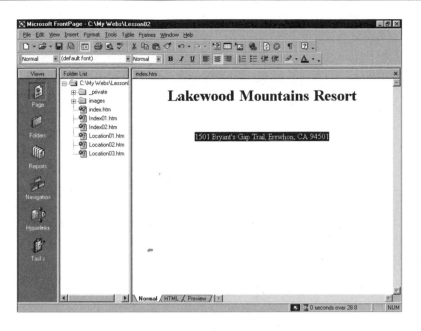

B

Bold

Save

7   On the Formatting toolbar, click the Bold button.

FrontPage applies bold formatting to the selected text.

8   On the toolbar, click the Save button.

FrontPage saves your changes.

Adding, Formatting, and Previewing a Marquee

You can easily add an impressive feature to the Lakewood Mountains Resort home page. A scrolling *marquee* displays text that slowly moves across the screen. This provides an eye-catching way to showcase a marketing message for Web site visitors. But use marquees and other animations sparingly. Numerous studies of Web users have noted that many people find Web sites that have excessive motion, animation, and blinking to be annoying.

You can adjust the speed and direction of a marquee's text movement, as well as the font, size, and style of the text.

Add a marquee

If you are not working through this lesson sequentially, follow the steps in "Import the Lesson 2 Practice Web" earlier in this lesson, drag the file Index01.htm from the Folder List into the Navigation view, and double-click its icon.

In this exercise, you add a marquee to the Lakewood Mountains Resort home page. You then adjust the scrolling speed and format the text.

1 Click the line below the address line.

FrontPage moves the insertion point to the next line. Notice that the insertion point is now aligned with the Web page's left margin.

2 On the Insert menu, point to Component, and then click Marquee.

FrontPage displays the Marquee Properties dialog box.

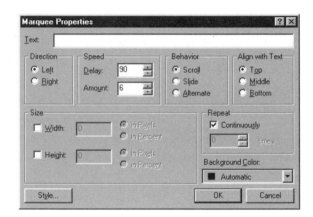

3 Type the following in the Text text box:

Welcome to Lakewood Mountains Resort, your luxury vacation retreat! Come home to: Spacious rooms. Fine food. Golf. Tennis. Swimming. Boating and fishing. Special programs for kids. And surprisingly low rates!

4 Click OK.

FrontPage places the marquee on your Web page. Only part of the text is visible, and it isn't scrolling. The text will scroll to the left when the page is displayed in a Web browser. You'll preview the marquee later in this lesson.

Customize the marquee

In this exercise, you change the width and background color of the marquee.

1 Right-click the marquee.

A shortcut menu appears.

Creating a Web Site

❷ On the shortcut menu, click Marquee Properties.

FrontPage displays the Marquee Properties dialog box.

❸ In the Size section of the dialog box, click the Width check box, double-click the Width check box, type **400**, and verify that In Pixels is selected.

The marquee will now have a width of 400 pixels.

❹ Click the Background Color drop-down arrow.

The Background Color palette expands.

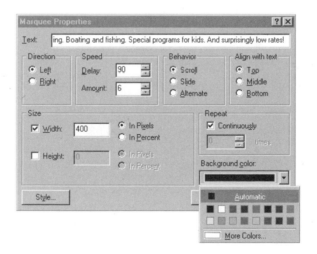

❺ Click the Yellow color tile.

The Background Color palette closes.

❻ Click OK.

FrontPage closes the Marquee Properties dialog box and changes the background color of the marquee to yellow.

Format the marquee text and save your work

In this exercise, you change the font and size of the marquee text.

1 Right-click the marquee, and then click Font on the shortcut menu.
FrontPage displays the Font dialog box.

In the Font dialog box, you can also click the Character Spacing tab to change the spacing or vertical position of the text in the marquee.

2 In the Font list, click Arial.
FrontPage displays a sample of the Arial font in the Preview pane.

3 In the Size list, click 4 (14 pt).
The preview text increases in size to 14 points.

tip

Points measure the height of text characters: there are 72 points per inch. Thus, 72-point type is one inch high, 12-point type is one-sixth of an inch high, and 14-point type is slightly less than one-fifth of an inch high.

4 Click OK.
FrontPage displays the marquee text in its new font and size.

5 On the toolbar, click the Save button.
FrontPage saves the Lakewood Mountains Resort home page.

Save

Preview your Web page

In this exercise, you preview the Lakewood Mountains Resort home page.

❶   Click the Preview tab at the bottom of the FrontPage window.

FrontPage displays a preview of the Web page. Although this provides you with a quick look at a Web page's appearance, it doesn't show how the page will look when loaded in a Web browser. Notice that the marquee text scrolls from right to left.

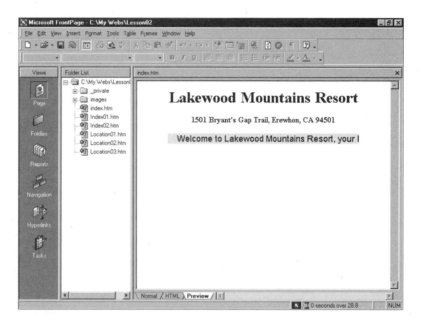

*Preview
In Browser*

Close

❷   On the toolbar, click the Preview In Browser button.

FrontPage displays the Web page in your default Web browser.

❸   Click the Close button at the top-right corner of the Web browser window.

Your Web browser closes and FrontPage is redisplayed.

❹   On the Views bar, click the Navigation icon.

FrontPage displays the Web structure.

Adding Web Pages

A Web can have just a single Web page. For a personal Web, you might consider this. But the Lakewood Mountains Resort Web needs several pages. You'll find that, with FrontPage, adding pages is easy to do.

To add a page, you can either create a new page or import an existing page. If you choose to create a new page, you can do so in most views. If you create a new page with your Web displayed in Navigation view (the view displayed when you click the Navigation icon on the Views bar), FrontPage creates a blank page and adds it to your Web.

There's an advantage in creating a page while your Web is shown in Page view (the view displayed when you click the Page icon on the Views bar). If you create a page in this view, you can use FrontPage's Web page wizards and templates. If you create a page in other views, it is a new blank page.

Just like the templates for Web sites, the templates for Web *pages* are pre-designed Web page blueprints for specific purposes. When you create a page with the Guest Book template, for example, the new page contains features and layout needed for a Web site guest book, as shown in the illustration. You simply add your own text and the page is ready to be used.

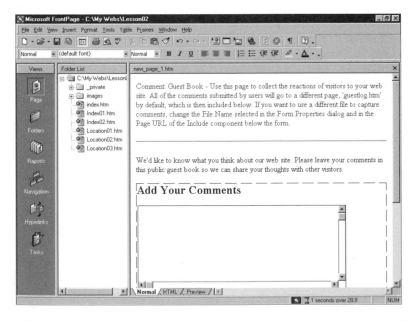

When creating the Web for Lakewood Mountains Resort, you'll create new pages in both Navigation and Page view, and you'll import an existing page.

Add a new Web page in Navigation view

If you are not working through this lesson sequentially, follow the steps in "Import the Lesson 2 Practice Web" earlier in this lesson, and drag the file Index01.htm from the Folder List into Navigation view.

In this exercise, you create a new page in Navigation view, and then delete it from your Web.

1   Make sure your home page is selected in Navigation view. On the File menu, point to New, and then click Page.

FrontPage creates a new Web page and adds it to the Web's tree diagram as a child of the home page.

2   Click the new page, and then press Delete. If the Delete Page dialog box appears, click the Delete This Page From The Web option, and click OK.

FrontPage deletes the new Web page and its link to the home page.

Add a new Web page in Page view

FrontPage uses the terms "parent" and "child" to differentiate between upper-level and lower-level Web pages.

In this exercise, you switch to Page view and browse through page templates before creating a new Web page.

1   On the Views bar, click the Page icon.

FrontPage displays the Web page in Page view.

2   On the File menu, point to New, and then click Page.

FrontPage displays the New dialog box.

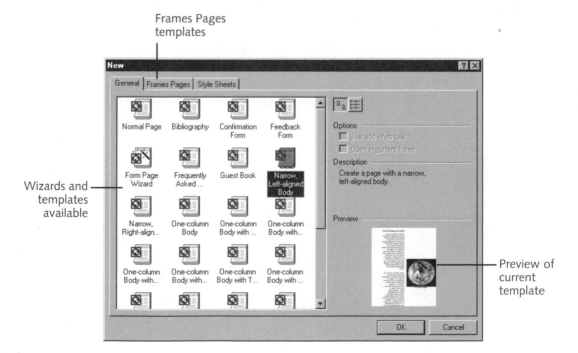

Frames Pages templates

Wizards and templates available

Preview of current template

❸ Click the icon for the Narrow, Left-Aligned Body template.

FrontPage displays the Web page layout in the Preview pane.

❹ Click the Frames Pages tab at the top of the dialog box.

FrontPage displays available templates for frames pages.

You'll learn how to create frames pages in Lesson 8, "Using Frames."

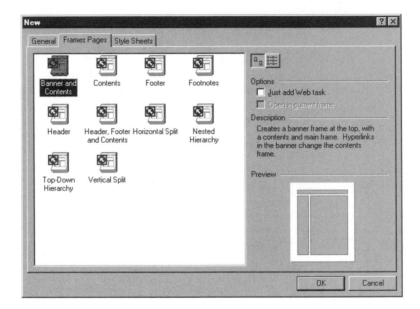

❺ Click the General tab, click the Normal Page template, and then click OK.

FrontPage creates a new, blank Web page and displays it in Page view.

Save

❻ On the toolbar, click the Save button to display the Save As dialog box.

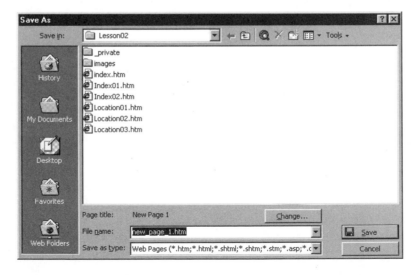

⑦ In the File Name text box, type **Location.htm**, and then click Save.

FrontPage saves the new Web page and adds it to the Folder List.

Save

⑧ On the toolbar, click the Save button.

FrontPage saves your changes to the Web.

New

tip

You can also create a new page by clicking the New button at the left end of the toolbar. Click the drop-down arrow to view a menu of options, including New Web.

Import a Web page

In this exercise, you import an existing Web page into the Lakewood Mountains Resort Web.

❶ On the Views bar, click the Navigation icon.

❷ On the File menu, click Import.

The Import dialog box appears.

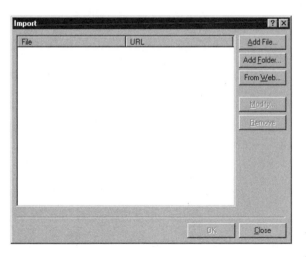

❸ Click the Add File button.

FrontPage displays the Add File To Import List dialog box.

④ Click the Look In drop-down arrow, browse to the FrontPage 2000 SBS Practice folder, double-click it, and then double-click the Extras folder.

The Extras folder opens and displays a file list.

⑤ Click the file named Recreati.htm, and then click the Open button.

FrontPage adds the file to the import list.

Press Ctrl while you click to select all three files.

⑥ Use the same method to add the files Boat_trips.jpg, Pool01.jpg, and Tennis_courts.jpg to the import list.

⑦ Click OK.

FrontPage imports the Web page and photo files into your Web. Notice that they now appear in the Folder List.

⑧ In the Folder List, double-click Recreati.htm.

FrontPage displays the Recreation Web page.

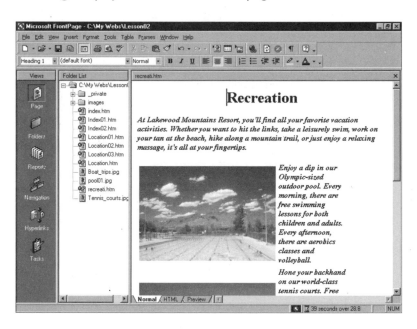

Save

⑨ On the toolbar, click the Save button.

FrontPage saves your changes.

Inserting a File into a Web Page

It's easy enough to enter Web page text in FrontPage. But what if you used Microsoft Word to write a description of Lakewood Mountains Resort? Of course, you could print the document and retype the text in FrontPage. But it's easier to insert the Word document's contents directly into a Web page.

Using FrontPage, you can insert the following types of files into Web pages.

- Microsoft Word documents.
- RTF (Rich Text Format) documents.
- TXT (plain text, or ASCII) files.
- Worksheets from Microsoft Excel and Lotus 1-2-3.
- WordPerfect 5.*x* and 6.*x* documents.
- HTML (Web page) files.

Insert a Microsoft Word document into a Web page

In this exercise, you insert the contents of an existing Microsoft Word document into a Web page.

① In the Folder List, double-click the file Location01.htm.

FrontPage displays the page (a blank Web page) in Page view.

② On the Insert menu, click File.

FrontPage displays the Select File dialog box. Navigate to the Extras folder within the FrontPage 2000 SBS Practice folder.

If an alert box is displayed notifying you that this feature is not installed, insert the Microsoft Office 2000 CD 1 or FrontPage 2000 CD in your CD-ROM drive, and click Yes.

③ Click the Files Of Type drop-down arrow, and click Word 97-2000 (*.doc).

There is only one Word document in the folder: Location.doc.

④ Click Location.doc, and then click the Open button.

FrontPage imports the text and inserts it on the Location01.htm page. Notice that the document's formatting, such as the bold type, has been preserved.

Save

⑤   On the toolbar, click the Save button.

FrontPage saves the Web page.

Changing Web Page Properties

Web page properties include a page's title, location, and summary. You can change a Web page's properties even after it has been created in FrontPage.

View and change the properties of a Web page

If you are not working through this lesson sequentially, follow the steps in "Import the Lesson 2 Practice Web" earlier in this lesson.

In this exercise, you view and change the properties of the Location Web page.

❶   In the Folder List, right-click Location02.htm, and then click Properties on the shortcut menu.

FrontPage displays the Location02.htm Properties dialog box.

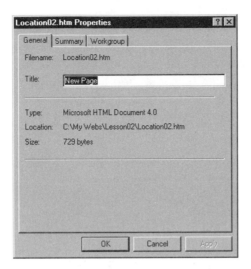

2 In the Title text box, type **Location**, and then click the Summary tab.

FrontPage displays the Summary section of the dialog box. In the Comments text box, you can type an explanation of the purpose of the current page.

3 Click OK.

FrontPage changes the title of the Web page.

4 On the toolbar, click the Save button.

FrontPage saves the Location page with its new title.

Save

One Step Further

Organizing Your Web

Although you now have three pages (the Index page, the Location page, and the Recreation page) in the Web site for Lakewood Mountains Resort, they aren't arranged in any particular structure. You know that the home page is the "starting" page, but beyond that, there's no organization.

In FrontPage, you can structure your Web by dragging Web page files into the Navigation view's tree diagram. There are many good reasons to do this. First, it makes your Web structure easier to understand. Instead of having to remember which Web pages link to which, you can simply look at the tree diagram.

Another reason has to do with designing your site. You can make FrontPage set up navigation bars to link all the pages displayed in Navigation view. Navigation bars use the information in the tree diagram to link pages. If the tree diagram of your Web isn't accurate, navigation bars won't work correctly.

Organize your Web

If you are not working through this lesson sequentially, follow the steps in "Import the Lesson 2 Practice Web" earlier in this lesson.

In this exercise, you create a navigation structure for the Lakewood Mountains Resort Web.

❶ On the Views bar, click the Navigation icon.

Only the home page is displayed in Navigation view.

❷ Drag the file Location01.htm from the Folder List into Navigation view below the home page.

A line connects the home page to the Location page.

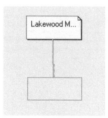

❸ Release the mouse button.

FrontPage makes the Location page into a child page (lower-level page) of the home page.

Finish the lesson

❶ On the File menu, click Close Web.

❷ If FrontPage prompts you to save changes, click the Yes button.

FrontPage saves your changes and closes the Lesson02 Web.

Lesson 2 Quick Reference

To	Do this	Button
Preview a Web page	Display the page in Page view and click the Preview tab at the bottom of the FrontPage window. *Or* click the Preview In Browser button on the toolbar.	

Lesson 2 Quick Reference

To	Do this
Create a Web	On the File menu, point to New, and click Web. Click the icon for the desired wizard or template. In the Specify The Location Of The New Web text box, type the name of the new Web and click OK. Use the Next button to work through the wizard dialog boxes, making selections as desired, and then click the Finish button.
Create a blank Web page	Display the Web in Navigation view. On the File menu, point to New, and then click Page.
Create a Web page using a wizard or template	Display the Web in Page view. On the File menu, point to New, and then click Page. In the dialog box, click the wizard or template you want to use, and click OK.
Enter and format text on a Web page	Double-click the Web page in the Folder List. In Page view, type and format text just as you would in Microsoft Word.
Add a marquee	Display the Web page in Page view and click the location where you want the marquee. On the Insert menu, point to Component, and then click Marquee. Type the marquee text, and then click OK.
Change marquee properties	Right-click the marquee and click Marquee Properties on the shortcut menu. Enter new properties as desired, and then click OK.
Change a Web page's properties	Right-click the Web page in the Folder List, and then click Properties. Use the General, Summary, or Workgroup tabs to enter or select new properties as desired. Click OK.
Import a Web page	On the File menu, click Import, and then click the Add File button. Browse to the file, click it, and click Open. Click OK.
Insert a file into a Web page	Display the Web page in Page view, and on the Insert menu, click File. Browse to the location of the file to insert, click the Files Of Type drop-down arrow, and then click the desired file type. Click the file to insert, and then click Open.
Organize a Web	Display the Web in Navigation view. Drag Web pages from the Folder List to form a tree diagram of the Web structure.

3

Linking
Web Pages

**ESTIMATED
TIME
30 min.**

In this lesson you will learn how to:

✔ *Create text hyperlinks between Web pages.*

✔ *Link to Web pages on the Internet.*

✔ *Create electronic mail links.*

✔ *Edit hyperlinks.*

✔ *Create Web page bookmarks.*

✔ *Create image map hyperlinks.*

Your client meeting with Lakewood Mountains Resort was a success: the resort manager was enthusiastic about the prototype Web site you created in Lesson 2. But she had a question: "Aren't the Web pages supposed to be linked together? I thought a user should be able to jump from one page to another by clicking text on the Web page."

You explain that Web pages can contain *hyperlinks,* which tell a Web browser to jump to another page on the Web site or on the Internet. She seems satisfied with that answer, which is lucky for you. Although you've used hyperlinks while surfing the Web, you have never created any. You'll soon learn that Microsoft FrontPage 2000 makes creating hyperlinks quick and easy.

In this lesson, you will learn how to create several kinds of hyperlinks. You will create text hyperlinks between Web pages, link to pages on the Internet, and create e-mail links. You will learn how to create and use bookmarks on your Web pages. Finally, you will create an image map hyperlink.

Creating Text Hyperlinks

A hyperlink is an HTML instruction embedded in a Web page. The instruction tells a Web browser to display another file or Web page when the visitor clicks the corresponding text or graphic. The newly displayed file can be a Web page on the World Wide Web, a Web page on a corporate intranet, or a file stored locally on the user's computer.

Pointing Hand

Each hyperlink has two parts: the hyperlink itself, and the *target,* which is the file displayed when a visitor clicks the hyperlink. When a visitor moves the mouse pointer over a hyperlink, it changes from its normal shape to a pointing hand. This tells the visitor that the pointer is over a hyperlink. The status bar at the bottom of the visitor's Web browser usually displays the address of the target. Without Microsoft FrontPage, creating hyperlinks can be complicated. But with FrontPage, you hardly need to worry about any of this. To create hyperlinks, you just point and click. FrontPage takes care of the details.

Import the Lesson 3 practice Web

In this exercise, you create a new Web based on the files in the Lesson03 folder in the FrontPage 2000 SBS Practice folder. You will use this Web for all the exercises in Lesson 3.

1 On the File menu, point to New, and then click Web.

FrontPage displays the New dialog box.

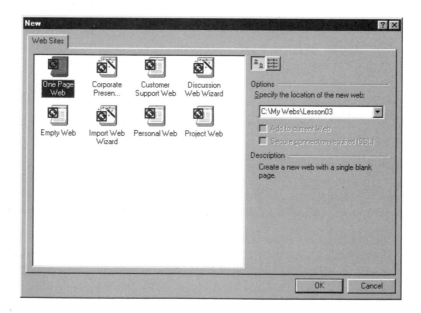

If your hard disk is not drive C, substitute the appropriate drive letter in step 2.

2 Click the Import Web Wizard icon. In the Specify The Location Of The New Web text box, delete the default text and type **C:\My Webs\Lesson03**, and click OK.

FrontPage displays the first Import Web Wizard dialog box.

3 Click the From A Source Directory Of Files option, click the Include Subfolders check box, and click the Browse button.

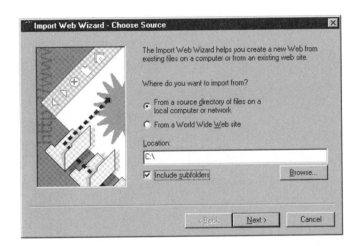

4 Browse to the Lesson03 folder in the FrontPage 2000 SBS Practice folder, and click OK.

5 Click Next twice, and then click Finish.

FrontPage creates a new Web based on the practice files and places it in the Lesson03 folder.

tip

If you need to quit FrontPage before you finish these exercises, here's a quick way to open the Lesson03 Web again. On the File menu, point to Recent Webs, and then click Lesson03.

New!
2000

Linking Web Pages

3

Link to a Web page in your current Web

In this exercise, you create a hyperlink between the Lakewood Mountains Resort home page and the Recreation page.

1 In the Folder List, double-click the file Index.htm.

FrontPage displays the home page in Page view.

2 On the home page, select the word *Recreation*.

3 On the Insert menu, click Hyperlink.

FrontPage displays the Create Hyperlink dialog box.

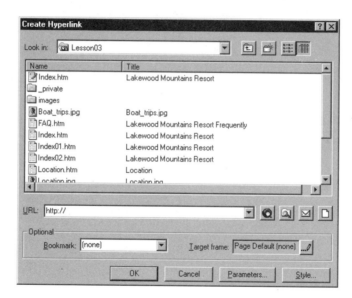

The shortcut key for inserting a hyperlink is Ctrl+K.

4 Click Recreati.htm in the file list.

FrontPage displays *Recreati.htm* in the URL text box. This is the Web page address for the hyperlink.

5 Click OK. Deselect the word *Recreation* by clicking any blank area of the home page.

FrontPage creates the hyperlink. Notice that the word *Recreation* is now underlined, indicating that it is a hyperlink.

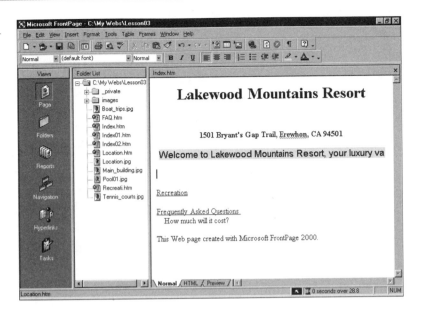

6 On the toolbar, click the Save button.

FrontPage saves your changes.

Save

tip

When you move the mouse over a hyperlink, FrontPage displays the link target address on the status bar, at the lower-right corner of your screen. You can check the functioning of your hyperlink by holding down Ctrl and clicking the link. FrontPage then displays the target page. In a later exercise, you will preview your links in your Web browser.

Link by dragging

In this exercise, you create a hyperlink by dragging a Web page from the Folder List onto the Web page displayed in Page view.

1 In the Folder List, click Location.htm.

2 Drag Location.htm so that it is just above the Recreation hyperlink, and then release the mouse button.

FrontPage creates a hyperlink to the Location page.

3 Press Ctrl and click the new Location link.

FrontPage displays the Location page.

4 In the Folder List, double-click Index.htm.

FrontPage redisplays the home page.

Save

5 On the toolbar, click the Save button.

FrontPage saves your changes.

Link to a Web page on the Internet

In this exercise, you create a hyperlink to a Web page on the Internet.

1 If necessary, connect to the Internet, and then switch back to FrontPage.

2 Select the word *Microsoft* in the last line on the home page, and then on the Insert menu, click Hyperlink.

FrontPage displays the Create Hyperlink dialog box.

Web Browser

3 Click the Web Browser button to link to a Web page on the Internet.

FrontPage opens your Web browser and instructs you to browse to the Web page you want to link.

4 In the Address bar of the Web browser, type *www.microsoft.com/frontpage* and press Enter.

Your Web browser connects to the Microsoft Web site and displays the FrontPage home page.

5 Press Alt+Tab on your keyboard to switch from your browser to FrontPage.

In the URL text box, FrontPage displays the Web address of the Microsoft FrontPage home page, as shown in the illustration.

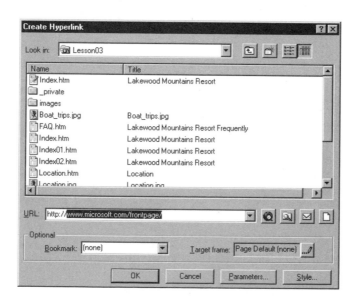

6 Click OK.

FrontPage creates the hyperlink.

7 On the toolbar, click the Save button.

FrontPage saves your changes.

Save

Test your hyperlinks

In this exercise, you test the hyperlinks you created on the Lakewood Mountains Resort home page.

1 If necessary, connect to the Internet, and then switch back to FrontPage.

2 On the toolbar, click the Preview In Browser button.

FrontPage displays the home page in your Web browser.

Preview In Browser

3 Click the *Location* hyperlink.

Your Web browser displays the Location page.

4 On the toolbar of your Web browser, click the Back button.

Your Web browser returns to the Lakewood Mountains Resort home page.

Back

5 Click the *Recreation* hyperlink.

Your Web browser displays the Recreation page.

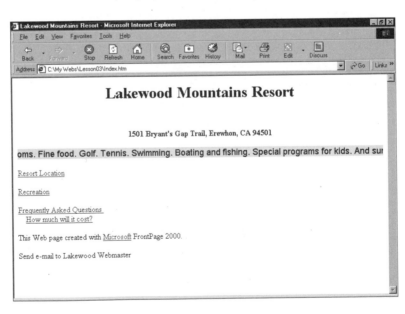

6 On the toolbar of your Web browser, click the Back button.

Your Web browser redisplays the Lakewood Mountains Resort home page.

Back

7   Click the *Microsoft* hyperlink.

FrontPage displays the Microsoft FrontPage home page in your Web browser.

8   Click the Close button at the top-right corner of your Web browser window.

Your Web browser closes, and FrontPage is redisplayed.

Close

Different Kinds of Hyperlinks

You can create several kinds of hyperlinks in the Create Hyperlinks dialog box.

You can also type the target address of the new hyperlink in the URL text box to create any kind of hyperlink.

Click	Name	To create a hyperlink
A file in the Folder List		To another page in your Web.
	Web Browser	To a file on the Internet.
	Local File	To a file on your own computer.
	E-mail	That sends e-mail.
	New	To a new Web page and link to it.

Creating a Link to an Electronic Mail Address

Hyperlinks can do more than just display a Web page or file. They also provide a way for Web site visitors to send electronic mail to addresses specified in hyperlinks. When a visitor clicks an e-mail hyperlink, the Web browser launches the visitor's e-mail program and displays a message composition window with the e-mail address already entered. The visitor then writes and sends the e-mail message normally.

For the Lakewood Mountains Resort home page, you want to enable visitors to send e-mail to the resort's Web site administrator, so you'll create a link to the Web administrator's e-mail address.

Create an electronic mail link

If you are not working through this lesson sequentially, follow the steps in "Import the Lesson 3 Practice Web" earlier in this lesson, and in the Folder List, double-click Index01.htm.

In this exercise, you create a hyperlink that enables Web page visitors to send electronic mail to the Web site administrator.

① Click the empty line below the Microsoft hyperlink.

② Type **Send e-mail to Lakewood Webmaster**, and then select the words *Lakewood Webmaster*.

③ On the Insert menu, click Hyperlink.

FrontPage displays the Create Hyperlink dialog box.

④ In the Create Hyperlink dialog box, click the E-mail button.

FrontPage displays the Create E-mail Hyperlink dialog box.

E-mail

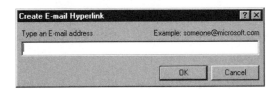

⑤ In the text box, type your own e-mail address, and then click OK.

The Create E-mail Hyperlink dialog box closes and the Create Hyperlink dialog box is again visible. Notice that the URL contains the text *mailto:* followed by your e-mail address.

⑥ Click OK.

FrontPage creates the new e-mail hyperlink.

Save

⑦ On the toolbar, click the Save button.

FrontPage saves your changes.

Editing Hyperlinks

Just like many other things in the modern world, hyperlinks often change. The name of a Web page file might change, it might be moved to a different Web site, or it might be deleted altogether. When such a change occurs, you need to change any hyperlinks that connect to the target file. Fortunately, changing a hyperlink in FrontPage is just as easy as creating it in the first place.

Change a hyperlink

If you are not working through this lesson sequentially, follow the steps in "Import the Lesson 3 Practice Web" earlier in this lesson, and in the Folder List, double-click Index01.htm.

In this exercise, you change the target Web page of the Lakewood Frequently Asked Questions hyperlink and then change the text of the Location hyperlink.

1 Right-click the Frequently Asked Questions hyperlink.

FrontPage displays a shortcut menu.

2 Click Hyperlink Properties.

FrontPage displays the Edit Hyperlink dialog box. Notice that the Frequently Asked Questions link has the Location page as its target in the URL text box. The Location page is an incorrect target for this link.

3 Click FAQ.htm in the file list, and then click OK.

FrontPage changes the target page to FAQ.htm.

4 Click any blank area of the page to deselect the link, and then check the Frequently Asked Questions link by pressing Ctrl and clicking the link.

FrontPage displays the Frequently Asked Questions page.

Close

5 Click the Close button at the top-right corner of the FAQ page.

FrontPage closes the FAQ page and displays the Index page.

6 Double-click the Location hyperlink, and then type **Resort Location**.

The new text replaces the old text, leaving the hyperlink intact.

Save

7 On the toolbar, click the Save button.

FrontPage saves your changes.

Delete a hyperlink

In this exercise, you delete a hyperlink but leave its Web page text intact.

1   Right-click the Lakewood Webmaster hyperlink.

FrontPage displays a shortcut menu.

2   On the shortcut menu, click Hyperlink Properties.

FrontPage displays the Edit Hyperlink dialog box. The URL text is selected.

3   Press Delete.

FrontPage deletes the URL text from the text box.

4   Click OK.

FrontPage deletes the hyperlink from the Web page text. Notice that the text is no longer underlined.

5   On the toolbar, click the Save button.

FrontPage saves your changes.

Save

> ## tip
> You can also delete a hyperlink by deleting the text on the Web page that contains the hyperlink.

Creating Bookmarks on a Web Page

Normally, when visitors click a hyperlink to a Web page, their browsers display only as much of the page as will fit in the browser window. If the Web page is longer than will fit on the screen, visitors must scroll down the page to see the rest of its content. For long Web pages, this can get to be a considerable chore.

Bookmarks can help with this problem. In FrontPage, a bookmark is a link to a specific location on a Web page. Lakewood Mountains Resort's Frequently Asked Questions (FAQ) page is very long, so you decide to insert a few bookmarks to make things easier for Web site visitors.

Create bookmarks

If you are not working through this lesson sequentially, follow the steps in "Import the Lesson 3 Practice Web" earlier in this lesson.

In this exercise, you create bookmarks on the Lakewood Mountains Resort's Frequently Asked Questions (FAQ) Web page.

1   In the Folder List, double-click the file FAQ.htm.

FrontPage displays the FAQ page in Page view.

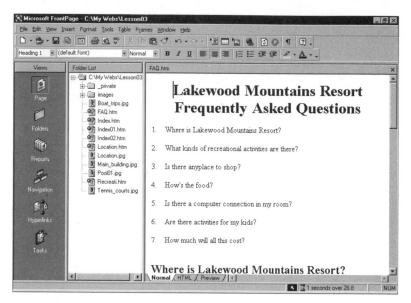

② Scroll down to the end of the FAQ page.

FrontPage displays the question *How much will all this cost?* and its answer.

③ Select the question text *How much will all this cost?*

tip

You aren't required to select text for a bookmark. You can simply place the insertion point where you want the bookmark, click Bookmark on the Insert menu, type a name for the bookmark, and click OK.

④ On the Insert menu, click Bookmark.

FrontPage displays the Bookmark dialog box.

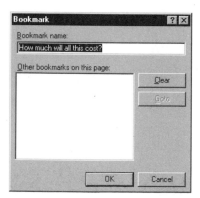

5 Click OK, and then deselect the question text by clicking any blank area of the FAQ page.

FrontPage creates the bookmark. Notice that the text is now underlined with a broken line. The broken underline distinguishes it from the solid underline displayed by a hyperlink.

6 Scroll up to the paragraph with the heading *How's the food?*, and select the question *How's the food?* On the Insert menu, click Bookmark.

FrontPage displays the Bookmark dialog box.

7 In the Bookmark dialog box, click OK.

FrontPage inserts another bookmark on the FAQ page.

8 Deselect the question text by clicking any blank area of the FAQ page, and then on the toolbar, click the Save button.

FrontPage saves the FAQ page with the new bookmarks.

Save

Link to a bookmark on the same Web page

In this exercise, you link from one location on a Web page to a bookmark at another location on the same Web page.

1 Scroll to the numbered list of questions at the top of the FAQ page.

2 Select the text *How's the food?*

3 On the Insert menu, click Hyperlink, and then click FAQ.htm in the dialog box's file list.

4 Click the Bookmark drop-down arrow, click *How's the food?*, and click OK.

FrontPage inserts the hyperlink.

5 On the toolbar, click the Save button.

FrontPage saves your changes.

Save

Link from another Web page to a bookmark

In this exercise, you create a link from a Web page to a bookmark on another Web page.

1 In the Folder List, double-click the file Index.htm.

FrontPage displays the home page in Page view.

2 Select the text *How much will it cost?*

3 On the Insert menu, click Hyperlink.

FrontPage displays the Create Hyperlink dialog box.

4 In the file list, click FAQ.htm, and then click the Bookmark drop-down arrow at the bottom of the dialog box.

FrontPage displays a list of bookmarks on the FAQ page.

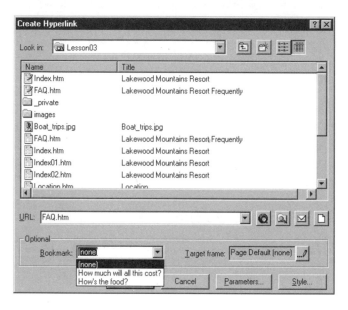

5 In the Bookmark list box, click *How much will all this cost?* and click OK.

The URL text box displays the target address and FrontPage inserts the hyperlink.

6 On the toolbar, click the Save button.

FrontPage saves your changes.

Save

Test your bookmarks

In this exercise, you test the bookmarks you created in the previous exercises.

1 On the toolbar, click the Preview In Browser button.

FrontPage opens the home page in your Web browser.

Preview In Browser

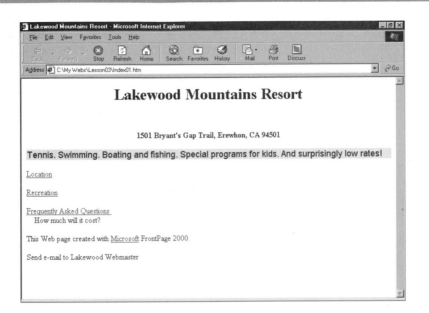

② Click the *How much will it cost?* hyperlink.

Your Web browser jumps down to the final question on the FAQ Web page.

③ Scroll to the top of the FAQ page.

④ Click the *How's the food?* hyperlink.

Your Web browser jumps down to the *How's the food?* bookmark.

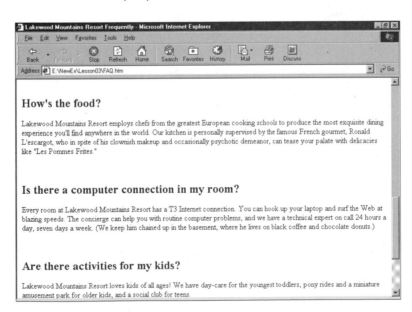

Close

Save

⑤ Click the Close button at the top-right corner of your Web browser window.

Your Web browser closes, and FrontPage is redisplayed.

⑥ On the toolbar, click the Save button.

FrontPage saves your changes.

Delete a bookmark

In this exercise, you delete a bookmark from the FAQ page.

❶ In the Folder List, double-click the file FAQ.htm.

FrontPage displays the FAQ page in Page view.

❷ If necessary, scroll to display the *How's the food?* bookmark (not the hyperlink).

❸ Right-click the bookmark text.

A shortcut menu is displayed.

❹ On the shortcut menu, click Bookmark Properties.

FrontPage displays the Bookmark dialog box.

You can also right-click the bookmark text, click Bookmark Properties, and press Delete to delete a bookmark.

⑤ In the Other Bookmarks On This Page box, click *How's the food?*, and then click the Clear button.

FrontPage deletes the bookmark.

Save

⑥ On the toolbar, click the Save button.

FrontPage saves your changes.

One Step Further

Creating Image Map Hyperlinks

So far, you've created text hyperlinks for the Lakewood Mountains Resort Web site. The resort manager, however, would like the Web site to have more visual excitement. She's seen Web sites in which a visitor can click part of an image and be taken directly to the Web page connected with that part of the image.

You've heard about that feature. It's called an *image map*. FrontPage makes it easy to create image maps. All you have to do is insert an image on a Web page, draw *hotspots*, create a few hyperlinks, and you've got an image map.

Insert an image on a Web page

If you are not working through this lesson sequentially, follow the steps in "Import the Lesson 3 Practice Web" earlier in this lesson.

In this exercise, you insert an image of the hotel building on the Lakewood Mountains Resort home page in preparation for creating an image map.

1 In the Folder List, double-click the file Index.htm.

FrontPage displays the Lakewood Mountains Resort home page.

2 Click the line below the text *Lakewood Mountains Resort* and above the resort's address.

3 On the Insert menu, point to Picture, and then click From File.

FrontPage displays the Picture dialog box.

4 In the file list, click Main_building.jpg.

FrontPage displays a preview of the image in the preview pane.

⑤   Click OK.

FrontPage inserts the image at the location you selected.

Save

⑥   On the toolbar, click the Save button.

FrontPage saves your changes.

Create an image map

For a demonstration of how to create an image map, in the Multimedia folder on the Microsoft FrontPage 2000 Step by Step CD-ROM, double-click the ImageMap icon.

In this exercise, you draw hotspots on the resort image to create an image map.

❶   Click the resort image to select it.

FrontPage displays the Image toolbar along the bottom of the screen.

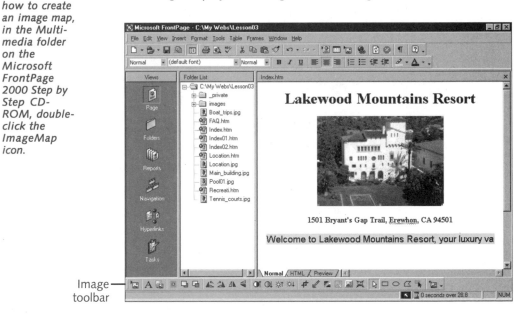

Image toolbar

Rectangular Hotspot

❷   On the Image toolbar, click the Rectangular Hotspot button.

❸   Hold down the mouse button, drag the mouse pointer to draw a rectangle on the grassy area in front of the hotel building, and release the mouse button.

FrontPage displays the Create Hyperlink dialog box.

❹   In the file list, click Recreati.htm, and then click OK.

FrontPage inserts a hyperlink for the image area you selected.

❺   Click the Rectangular Hotspot button, draw another rectangle on the hotel building, and then release the mouse button.

FrontPage displays the Create Hyperlink dialog box.

⑥ In the file list, click Location.htm, and then click OK.

FrontPage inserts another hyperlink for the image area you selected.

Save

⑦ On the toolbar, click the Save button.

FrontPage saves your changes.

Test the image map

In this exercise, you test the image map you created in the previous exercise.

Preview In Browser

① On the toolbar, click the Preview In Browser button.

FrontPage displays the home page in your Web browser.

② Move the mouse pointer over the image.

Over the hotspots, the mouse pointer turns from an arrow into a pointing hand, indicating the presence of hyperlinks.

Pointing Hand

③ Click the grassy area hotspot.

Your Web browser displays the Recreation page.

④ On the toolbar of your Web browser, click the Back button, and then click the hotel building hotspot.

Back

Your Web browser displays the Location page.

Finish the lesson

Close

❶   Click the Close button at the top-right corner of your Web browser window. Your Web browser closes and FrontPage reappears.

❷   On the File menu, click Close Web.

❸   For each page, if FrontPage prompts you to save changes, click Yes. FrontPage saves your changes and closes the Lesson03 Web.

Lesson 3 Quick Reference

To	Do this
Import a Web	On the File menu, point to New, and click Web. Click the Import Web Wizard icon, type the name of the folder for the new Web, and click OK. Click the From A Source Directory Of Files option to select it, click the Include Subfolders check box, and then click the Browse button. Browse to the folder that contains the files you want to import, and click OK. Click Next, click Next again, and then click Finish.
Create a text hyperlink	Select the hyperlink text, and on the Insert menu, click Hyperlink. If necessary, browse to the target file. Select the target file, and click OK.
Create a hyperlink by dragging	Display the Web page that will have the hyperlink in Page view. Drag a file from the Folder List to the desired location on the Web page and release the mouse button.
Change a hyperlink target	Right-click the hyperlink and click Hyperlink Properties. In the Edit Hyperlink dialog box, select the new hyperlink target, and click OK.
Change hyperlink text	Select the hyperlink text, and type the new text.
Delete a hyperlink	Right-click the hyperlink text, click Hyperlink Properties, and then press Delete. Click OK.
Create a bookmark	Select the bookmark text, on the Insert menu, click Bookmark, and then click OK.
Create a hyperlink to a bookmark	Select the hyperlink text, and then click Hyperlink on the Insert menu. If necessary, browse to the target file. Select the target file, click the Bookmark drop-down arrow, click the desired bookmark, and then click OK.

Lesson 3 Quick Reference

To	Do this	Button
Delete a bookmark	Right-click the bookmark text, click Bookmark Properties, and then click the Clear button.	
Create an e-mail hyperlink	Select the hyperlink text, and then on the Insert menu, click Hyperlink. Click the E-mail button, type the e-mail address, and click OK twice.	✉
Insert an image on a Web page	Place the insertion point in the desired location. On the Insert menu, point to Picture, and then click From File. If needed, browse to the location of the image file. Click the image file, and then click OK.	
Create an image map	Click the image on the Web page. On the Image toolbar, click the Rectangular Hotspot button and draw a hotspot on the image. In the Create Hyperlink dialog box, select the target file, and then click OK.	▢

Linking Web Pages

3

Review & Practice

> **You will review and practice how to:**
>
> ✔ Design a Web site.
> ✔ Create a Web site.
> ✔ Add pages to a Web site.
> ✔ Add and format text on a Web page.
> ✔ Add a marquee to a Web page.
> ✔ Create hyperlinks on a Web page.

Before you go on to Part 2, which covers FrontPage components, advanced Web page formatting, and multimedia, you should review the skills you've learned in Part 1 by working through this Review & Practice section. You will review how to design and create a Web site, add pages to a Web site, add and format text on a Web page, add a scrolling marquee to a Web page, and create hyperlinks.

Scenario

Your boss at Impact Public Relations is very impressed with your work on the Web site for Lakewood Mountains Resort. She's asked you to conduct a training session for some of the new account executives and teach them what you've learned about using Microsoft FrontPage. With the new people crowding around your desk, you explain the basics of Web site design and demonstrate how to create a Web site with FrontPage. You then add a Web page, add and format text, and show how to create a marquee. Finally, you create some simple hyperlinks.

Step 1:   Design a Web Site

You demonstrate how to design a Web site, and you lead your coworkers through the steps of defining its purposes, determining what pages are needed, and creating an empty Web site using a template. You show them how to use FrontPage's views of a Web site, close FrontPage, and get more ideas for a Web site from the World Wide Web.

1 Define the purposes of the Web site and determine what pages are needed for the site.

2 Start FrontPage.

3 In a folder named Review01, create an empty Web using the Empty Web template.

4 View the Web in Navigation view, Reports view, and Page view.

5 Close the Web.

6 On the World Wide Web, visit Microsoft's FrontPage home page at *www.microsoft.com/frontpage* to get additional ideas and information you can use in creating Web sites.

For more information about	See
Defining the purposes of a Web site	Lesson 1
Determining what pages are needed	Lesson 1
Starting FrontPage	Lesson 1
Using wizards and templates	Lesson 2
Creating a Web in FrontPage	Lessons 1 and 2
Using FrontPage views	Lesson 1
Closing FrontPage	Lesson 1
Getting Web design ideas and information	Lesson 1

Step 2:   Create a Web Site

As the training session continues, you demonstrate how to create a home page, how to add and format text on the page, and how to create a scrolling marquee. You then show your coworkers how to save a Web page, preview a Web, add more pages to a Web, change page properties, and import files into a Web. Finally, you demonstrate how to save a Web.

1 Add a home page to the empty Web you created in Step 1.

2 On the home page, add the heading **My FrontPage Demo** and add the body text **This is to show my coworkers how to create amazing Webs with FrontPage.**

3 Select the word *amazing* and italicize it.

4 Under the body text, create a marquee. Type the text **I'm turning into a real Web expert!** Make the text yellow on a blue background.

5 Save the home page as *Demo1.htm* and preview the Web in your Web browser.

6 On the Views bar, click the Page icon, and add another page to your Web. Save the page as *Demo2.htm* and title it *Another Demo Page*.

7 Change the title of your home page to *My First Demo Page*.

8 From the Lesson02 folder in the FrontPage 2000 SBS folder, import the Recreati.htm Web page.

For more information about	See
Creating a home page	Lesson 2
Adding text to a page	Lesson 2
Formatting text on a page	Lesson 2
Creating and formatting a marquee	Lesson 2
Saving a page	Lesson 2
Previewing a Web	Lesson 2
Adding a page	Lesson 2
Changing page properties	Lesson 2
Importing a file	Lesson 2

Step 3: Create Hyperlinks

Now that you've created some pages in the Web, you explain hyperlinks and you demonstrate how to insert them on Web pages, how to create links between pages in a Web, how to link to pages on the Internet, and how to create e-mail links, bookmarks, and an image map.

1 On the home page, type **Demo Page 2** and make the text into a hyperlink leading to the second page in your Web. On Demo2.htm, create a similar link that leads back to the home page.

2 Establish an Internet connection and, on the home page, create a hyperlink to *www.microsoft.com/frontpage*.

3 Create an e-mail hyperlink that will send messages to your own e-mail address.

4 From the Lesson03 folder in the FrontPage 2000 SBS Practice folder, import FAQ.htm and insert a bookmark on the heading *Is there anyplace to shop?*

❺ On the home page, create a hyperlink that leads to the bookmark on the FAQ page.

❻ From the Lesson03 folder in the FrontPage 2000 SBS Practice folder, import the file Main_Building.jpg and use it to create an image map on the home page with a link to the second page.

For more information about	See
Creating hyperlinks within a Web	Lesson 3
Creating hyperlinks to files on the Internet	Lesson 3
Creating e-mail hyperlinks	Lesson 3
Creating and using bookmarks	Lesson 3
Creating image maps	Lesson 3

Finish the Review & Practice

❶ Save your changes to the home page and the second page.

❷ Close the Review01 Web.

PART 2

Formatting and Enhancing Your Web Pages

4

Adding Style to Web Pages

**ESTIMATED
TIME
30 min.**

In this lesson you will learn how to:

✔ *Apply a FrontPage theme.*

✔ *Modify a FrontPage theme.*

✔ *Use FrontPage components.*

✔ *Modify component properties.*

✔ *Use Web page style sheets.*

The prototype Web site for Lakewood Mountains Resort is a big hit at your next meeting, but the client has a few requests. First, all Web pages on the Web site should have a nice color scheme and a consistent style or "look" for text, hyperlinks, buttons, banners, and other Web page elements. Second, each Web page should have a banner at the top, and the home page should show how many *hits*, or visitors, the Web site has received. Finally, each Web page should have a copyright notice.

You assure the client that Microsoft FrontPage 2000 makes it easy to add these features to the Web site. In this lesson, you will learn how to apply FrontPage *themes* to give a consistent look to all of your Web pages. You will also learn how to use FrontPage components to display hit counters, Web page banners, and other features. Finally, you will learn how to use Web page style sheets. Armed with themes and components, you prepare to make the changes requested by the client.

Understanding FrontPage Themes

FrontPage themes provide ready-to-use arrangements of stylish backgrounds and graphics for Web pages. You can apply a theme to an entire Web or just to an individual page. When you apply a theme to an entire Web, it gives a consistent look to all of the pages in your Web.

When you select a theme, all Web pages get the same color scheme, background, navigation bars, buttons, and other Web page elements. This gives your Web a polished, professional look with minimal time and effort. When you add new pages to your Web, FrontPage automatically creates them using the same theme.

Import the Lesson 4 practice Web

In this exercise, you create a new Web based on the files in the Lesson04 folder in the FrontPage 2000 SBS Practice folder. You will use this Web for all the exercises in Lesson 4.

① On the File menu, point to New, and then click Web.

FrontPage displays the New dialog box.

If your hard disk has a drive letter other than C, substitute the appropriate drive letter in step 2.

② Click the Import Web Wizard icon. In the Specify The Location Of The New Web text box, delete the default text and type **C:\My Webs\Lesson04**, and then click OK.

FrontPage displays the first Import Web Wizard dialog box.

③ Click the From A Source Directory Of Files option, click the Include Subfolders check box, and then click the Browse button.

④ Browse to the Lesson 04 folder in the FrontPage 2000 SBS Practice folder, and click OK.

⑤ Click Next twice, and then click Finish.

FrontPage creates a new Web based on the practice files and places it in the Lesson04 folder.

For a demonstration of how to apply a theme to a single Web page, in the Multimedia folder on the Microsoft FrontPage 2000 Step by Step CD-ROM, double-click the Theme icon.

Apply a theme to a single Web page

In this exercise, you view the themes included with FrontPage and apply the Expedition theme to a single page of your Web.

① In the Folder List, double-click the file Welcome.htm.

FrontPage displays the Web page.

❷   On the Format menu, click Theme.

       FrontPage displays the Themes dialog box.

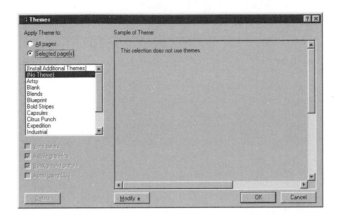

❸   In the Themes list at the left, click Artsy.

       FrontPage displays a sample of how Web page elements look with the Artsy
       theme.

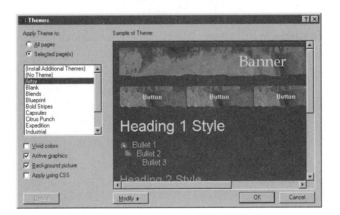

❹   In the Themes list, click Rice Paper.

       FrontPage displays a sample of how Web page elements look with the Rice
       Paper theme.

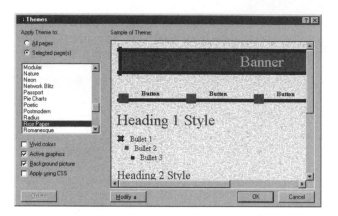

5   In the Themes list, click Expedition.

FrontPage displays a sample of how Web page elements look with the Expedition theme.

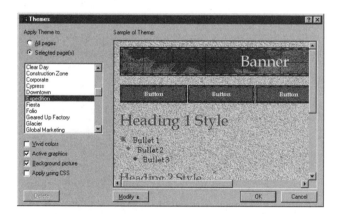

6   Click the Background Picture check box.

FrontPage displays a sample of the page without the background picture.

7   Click the Background Picture check box again.

FrontPage restores the background picture.

8   Click OK.

FrontPage applies the Expedition theme to the Welcome Web page, with the options you selected.

Save

9   On the toolbar, click the Save button.

FrontPage saves your changes to the Web page.

tip

You can apply a background image to a Web page without using a theme. To do so, display the Web page in Page view and click Background on the Format menu. In the Page Properties dialog box, click the Background tab, click the Background Picture check box, and click the Browse button. Browse to the image you want, and then click OK twice. Note that the image you select will appear as a repeating tile in the background of your Web page.

Apply a theme to a Web

In this exercise, you apply the Expedition theme to all the pages of the Lakewood Mountains Resort Web.

1   On the Format menu, click Theme.

FrontPage displays the Themes dialog box with the Expedition theme selected.

2   At the top-left corner of the dialog box, click the All Pages option, and then click OK.

FrontPage applies the Expedition theme to all the Web pages in the Lesson04 Web.

tip

To remove a theme from a Web page, display the Web page in Page view, and click Theme on the Format menu. In the Themes dialog box, click the Selected Pages option, click No Theme in the Themes list, and click OK. To remove a theme from an entire Web, click Theme on the Format menu, click the All Pages option, click No Theme in the Themes list, and then click OK.

Modify a theme

In this exercise, you modify the theme of the Lakewood Mountains Resort Web.

1   On the Format menu, click Theme.

FrontPage displays the Themes dialog box with a preview of the Web's current theme.

2 Click the Modify button.

The dialog box now displays a row of buttons labeled *What Would You Like To Modify?*

3 Click the Colors button, click the Custom tab, and then click the Item drop-down arrow.

The Item box expands and displays a list of Web page items whose color you can change.

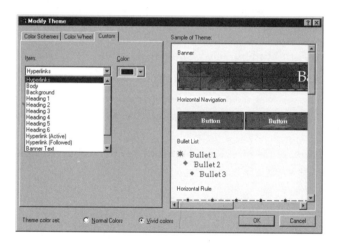

4 Click any blank area of the dialog box to close the drop-down list. Click Cancel, click the Graphics button, and then click the Item drop-down arrow.

FrontPage displays the Modify Theme dialog box with a list of graphic elements whose appearance you can change.

5 Click any blank area of the dialog box to close the drop-down list. Click Cancel, and then click Text.

FrontPage displays the Modify Theme dialog box with a list of the textual theme elements whose appearance you can change.

6 Click the Item drop-down arrow, click Heading 1, scroll down the Font list, and then click Comic Sans MS. Click OK.

FrontPage changes the font of the Heading 1 style to Comic Sans MS.

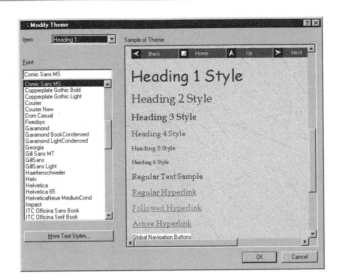

7 Click OK, and then click Cancel so you don't permanently modify the theme.

FrontPage closes the dialog box without saving your changes.

Delete a theme from a Web page

In this exercise, you delete a theme from the Welcome Web page.

1 If necessary, double-click Welcome.htm in the Folder List.

FrontPage displays the Welcome page in Page view.

2 On the Format menu, click Theme.

FrontPage displays the Themes dialog box. The Expedition theme is selected.

3 In the Apply Theme To section of the dialog box, if the Selected Page(s) option is not selected, click it.

FrontPage will apply any changes only to the currently displayed Web page.

4 In the Themes list, click No Theme, and then click OK.

FrontPage removes the theme from the Welcome page.

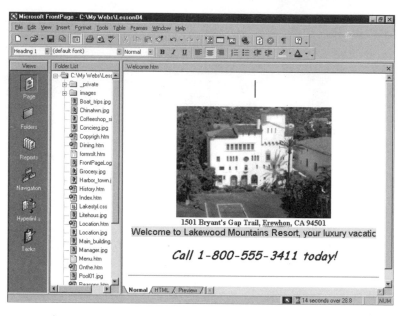

Save

Close

⑤   On the toolbar, click the Save button, and then click the Close button at the top-right corner of the Welcome page.

FrontPage saves your changes and closes the Welcome page.

Delete a theme from an entire Web

In this exercise, you delete a theme from an entire Web rather than a single page.

❶   On the Format menu, click Theme.

FrontPage displays the Themes dialog box. Expedition is selected.

❷   In the Apply Theme To section of the dialog box, make sure the All Pages option is selected.

FrontPage will apply any changes to all pages in the Web.

❸   In the Themes list, click No Theme, and then click OK.

FrontPage removes the theme from the entire Web.

Adding FrontPage Components

FrontPage components are ready-to-use programs that are activated when a user loads a page into a Web browser. They provide a quick and easy way to build features into Web pages without having to learn Web page scripting or ActiveX and Java programming. Some components included with FrontPage are summarized in the following table.

Component	Explanation
Comment	Inserts a comment into a Web page's HTML code to explain some aspect of the coding or design. The comment is invisible when the page is viewed in a browser, though it is visible in Page view. Useful for annotating the page as you work on it.
Page Banner*	Inserts a graphical banner at the top of a Web page.
Banner Ad Manager	Rotates the display of multiple images at specified intervals. Allows you to select the type of transition between banners (dissolve, horizontal blinds, and so on) and link banners to a Web page.
Hit Counter*	Displays the number of times a page has been visited, or "hit."
Hover Button	Inserts a link that displays a visual effect when the mouse pointer "hovers," or is positioned over it. Effects include changing color and appearing to be pressed like a button.
Marquee	Displays text that scrolls horizontally on the Web page.
Confirmation Field*	Confirms a user's entry on a Web page form.
Include Page	Inserts a Web page at a specified location inside another page. For example, you might insert a copyright page at the bottom of every page in your Web.
Scheduled Picture*	Displays a picture for a specified period of time and optionally replaces it with another picture. Useful for displaying time-critical information, such as a "New" icon on a new page.
Scheduled Include Page*	Inserts a Web page inside another page for a specified period of time and optionally replaces it at a specified time. Useful for displaying time-critical information, such as notification of a seasonal sale.
Substitution	Replaces a section of text with a specified value, such as another text string.
Categories	Inserts links to pages by category. Useful for creating tables of contents for pages of a certain type, such as Expense Reports or Planning.
Search Form*	Allows visitors to search the site for specified text. When you save a page with a Search form, FrontPage builds an index of the site. When users perform a search, FrontPage uses the index to create a list of hyperlinks to pages containing the word or phrase.
Table of Contents	Creates a table of contents for the Web site.

*Requires a Web server that has the FrontPage Server Extensions.

Adding Style to Web Pages

4

Add a Web page banner

If you are not working through this lesson sequentially, follow the steps in "Import the Lesson 4 Practice Web" earlier in this lesson.

In this exercise, you add a banner to the Welcome page of the Lakewood Mountains Resort Web site.

1 In the Folder List, double-click the file Welcome.htm.

FrontPage displays the Welcome page in Page view.

2 On the Format menu, click Theme. Click Expedition, and then click OK.

FrontPage applies the Expedition theme to the Welcome page.

3 If necessary, click the line above the hotel photo.

The insertion point moves to the line above the photo.

tip

To display banners properly, a Web page must meet two requirements. First, it must be included in a Web page hierarchy that you create in Navigation view. Second, the page must have a theme applied; otherwise the banner will appear as plain text.

4 On the Insert menu, click Page Banner.

FrontPage displays the Page Banner Properties dialog box.

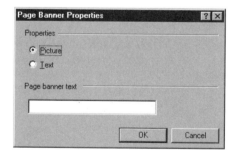

5 In the Page Banner Text box, type **Lakewood Mountains Resort**, and then click OK.

FrontPage displays the banner at the top of the Web page, but the banner text is not yet displayed.

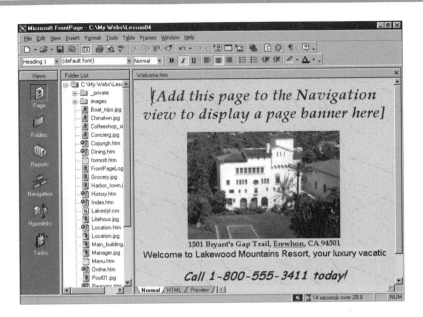

⑥ On the Views bar, click the Navigation icon.

FrontPage displays the Web in Navigation view. At present, only the Web's home page is shown in the hierarchy diagram.

⑦ Drag Welcome.htm from the Folder List into Navigation view until a line connects it to the home page, and release the mouse button.

The Welcome page is now linked to the home page.

⑧ In the Folder List, double-click the file Welcome.htm.

FrontPage displays the page. The banner text is now displayed correctly.

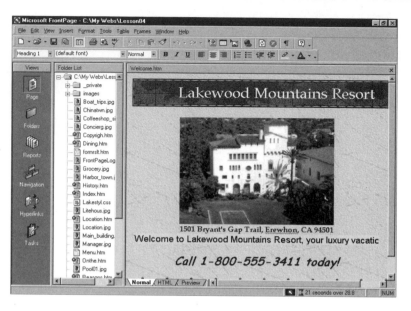

Save

❾ On the toolbar, click the Save button.

FrontPage saves your changes.

tip

If page banner text is not being displayed correctly, first right-click the banner and click Page Banner Properties on the shortcut menu. If the banner text in the dialog box is correct and the Picture option is selected, click Cancel, and then click the Navigation icon on the Views Bar. Verify that the Web page is linked into the Web hierarchy diagram.

Add a hit counter

In this exercise, you add a hit counter to the Welcome page. The hit counter will display the number of visitors to your site since it was installed or reset.

important

To publish and display a hit counter on your local computer, you must be running Microsoft Personal Web Server, which you can download from the Microsoft Web site. If you do not have the Personal Web Server installed, you can insert a hit counter on a page, but you cannot display it until you publish your Web to a Web server.

1 Click at the right end of the line *Call 1-800-555-3411 today!* and press Enter.

The cursor moves to a new line below the phone number.

2 On the toolbar, click the Font Size drop-down arrow, and click 3 (12pt).

FrontPage changes the current text size to 12 points.

3 Type **You are visitor number**, and then press the Spacebar.

FrontPage inserts a caption for the hit counter.

4 On the Insert menu, point to Component, and then click Hit Counter.

FrontPage displays the Hit Counter Properties dialog box.

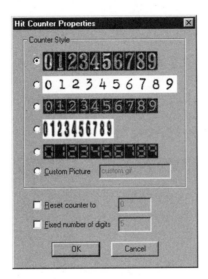

5 Click the option for the style you like best, click the Fixed Number Of Digits check box, and then click OK.

FrontPage inserts the hit counter at the selected location. However, the hit counter will not be displayed until you publish the Web.

Save

If you have not downloaded and installed the Microsoft Personal Web Server, stop after step 6.

6 On the toolbar, click the Save button.

FrontPage saves your changes.

7 On the File menu, click Publish Web, and then click the Options button.

FrontPage displays the Publish Web dialog box with the Options area visible.

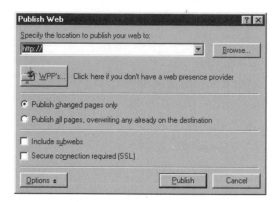

8 In the Specify The Location To Publish Your Web text box, type **http://localhost**.

This tells FrontPage that you want to publish your Web to your local hard disk drive.

9 Click the Publish All Pages option, and then click the Publish button.

FrontPage displays a dialog box indicating that you successfully published your Web to your local hard disk drive.

Depending on the speed of your computer and hard disk drive, publishing your Web could take a minute or two.

10 In the dialog box, click the text *Click Here to View Your Published Web Site*.

FrontPage opens the published Web site in your Web browser. Notice that the hit counter is partially visible at the bottom of the browser window.

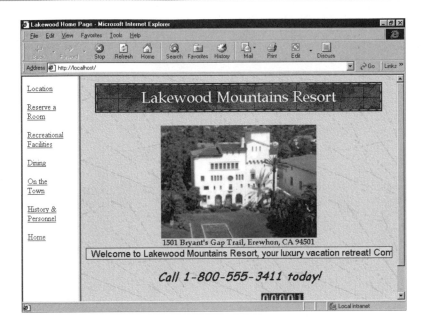

11 Scroll down in your Web browser to view the bottom of the Welcome page.

You can now see the hit counter and its caption.

Close

12 Click the Close button at the top-right corner of your Web browser window.

Your Web browser closes and the dialog box reappears in FrontPage.

13 Click the Done button.

The dialog box closes.

important

Once you publish your Web to a server, components such as the hit counter will require that the Web server have the FrontPage Server Extensions in order to work properly.

Include one Web page inside another

In this exercise, you include the Copyright page in the Lakewood Mountains Resort Welcome page.

1 Scroll down if necessary, and then click the line below the horizontal line at the bottom of the Web page.

FrontPage moves the insertion point to the bottom of the Web page.

② On the Insert menu, point to Component, and then click Include Page. FrontPage displays the Include Page Properties dialog box.

③ Click the Browse button, and in the file list, click Copyrigh.htm (the Copyright Web page).

④ Click OK twice.

The dialog boxes close and the Copyright page is inserted at the bottom of the Welcome page.

⑤ If necessary, scroll down to view the included Web page.

The included page contains copyright information, an e-mail link, and the "Site Created With Microsoft FrontPage" logo.

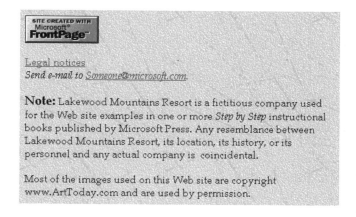

⑥ On the toolbar, click the Save button.

FrontPage saves your changes.

Save

One Step Further **Using Web Page Style Sheets**

Themes are just one way you can customize the appearance of your Web pages. Another way is to use *styles* and *style sheets*. A style is a set of characteristics (such as size, spacing, and color) that you apply to a Web page element, such as a heading. A style sheet is a collection of styles that you apply to an entire page.

Elements such as headings and text have a default appearance that depends partly on the user's Web browser and partly on the fonts installed on the user's computer. By applying styles or style sheets, you can often override these defaults and display the page precisely as you want.

FrontPage gives you three ways to apply styles. First, you can simply right-click a specific Web page element, click Properties on its shortcut menu, and change its appearance in the Properties dialog box. (This is called applying an inline style.) It applies the style changes only to the Web page element you selected; if you change the style of one body text paragraph, all other paragraphs on the page will remain unchanged.

Another way of applying styles is to create a page header style sheet. When you apply a style to an element (such as a heading or the body text) in a Web page header style sheet, it affects all elements of that type on the current page. For example, you might create a style for body text to make it 36 points in size, centered, red-colored, and using the Arial font. When you apply this style to a Web page, all of the body text on the page turns into 36-point, centered, red Arial text. To create a header style sheet, you click Style on the Format menu and then make the desired changes in the Style dialog box.

The third and most powerful way to apply styles is to create an external style sheet and link it to one or more Web pages on your Web site. This enables you to make the same style changes to multiple Web pages, but it is more difficult than the other methods. You can learn more about creating external style sheets on the Help menu or on the World Wide Web Consortium's site at *www.w3.org*.

tip
You'll sometimes hear style sheets called "Cascading Style Sheets" (CSS). This means that you can apply multiple style sheets to the same Web page, so that styles in a higher layer override styles in lower layers.

Create a header style sheet

If you are not working through this lesson sequentially, follow the steps in "Import the Lesson 4 Practice Web" earlier in this lesson.

In this exercise, you create a header style sheet for a Web page.

1 In the Folder List, double-click the file Reasons.htm.

FrontPage displays the Web page.

2 On the Format menu, click Style.

FrontPage displays the Style dialog box.

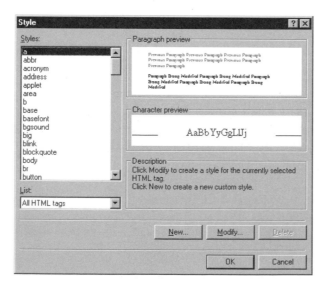

❸ In the Styles list, scroll down and click H1, and then click the Modify button.

The Modify Style dialog box appears.

❹ Click the Format button, and then click Font on the shortcut menu.

The Font dialog box appears.

❺ Click the Color drop-down arrow, click one of the Blue color tiles, and click OK twice.

FrontPage creates an H1 style and sets the text color to blue. The Style dialog box reappears.

❻ Click the List drop-down arrow and click All HTML Tags.

FrontPage redisplays the full list of Web page styles.

❼ In the Styles list, click H2, click the Modify button, click the Format button, and click Font on the shortcut menu.

FrontPage displays the Font dialog box.

❽ Click the Color drop-down arrow, click the Red color tile, click the All Caps check box to select it, and then click OK three times.

The dialog boxes close and FrontPage displays the style changes. Notice that the Heading 1 text is now blue, and the Heading 2 text is red and all uppercase.

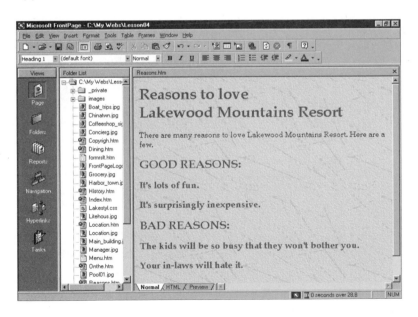

Finish the lesson

① On the File menu, click Close Web.

② For each page, if FrontPage prompts you to save changes, click Yes.

FrontPage saves your changes and closes the Lesson04 Web.

Lesson 4 Quick Reference

To	Do this
View FrontPage themes	On the Format menu, click Theme. In the Themes dialog box, click the desired theme and view it in the sample pane.
Apply a theme to an individual Web page	Display the page in Page view. On the Format menu, click Theme. In the Themes dialog box, click the Selected Pages option, and click the desired theme. Check the desired check boxes, and then click OK.
Apply a theme to an entire Web	On the Format menu, click Theme, click the All Pages option, and click the desired theme. Check the desired check boxes, and click OK.
Modify a theme	On the Format menu, click Theme. In the Themes dialog box, click the Modify button, and then click the button for the theme characteristic you want to modify. Make the desired changes in the Modify Theme dialog box, and then click OK. Click the Save As button, type a new theme name if desired, and click OK.
Insert a FrontPage component	Click the desired location for the component. On the Insert menu, point to Component, and click the desired component. Adjust the component properties as needed.
Insert a Web page banner	Display the Web page in Page view. On the Insert menu, click Page Banner. Type the Web page banner text, and click OK. Click the Navigation icon on the Views Bar and drag the Web page into the Web hierarchy diagram.
Insert a hit counter	Display the Web page in Page view and click at the desired location for the hit counter. Type a caption and press the Spacebar. On the Insert menu, point to Component, and then click Hit Counter. Adjust the hit counter style and properties, and then click OK.

Lesson 4 Quick Reference

To	Do this
Include a page in another Web page	If necessary, create the Web page you want to include. In Page view, display the Web page in which the included Web page will be inserted, and click the desired location. On the Insert menu, point to Component, and then click Include Page. Click Browse, browse to the Web page to be included, and click OK twice.
Create a header style	Display the desired Web page in Page view. On the Format menu, click Style. If needed, click the List drop-down arrow and click All HTML Tags to display all Web page styles in the Styles list. Click the style you want to modify, click the Modify button, click the Format button, and click the desired style attribute on the shortcut menu. Make the desired changes, and click OK three times.

5

Formatting Web Pages

ESTIMATED TIME 40 min.

In this lesson you will learn how to:

✔ *Create bulleted and numbered lists.*

✔ *Format bulleted and numbered lists.*

✔ *Use tables to arrange Web page elements.*

✔ *Format tables and table cells.*

✔ *Change Web page properties.*

As you refine your Web site for Lakewood Mountains Resort, you think about how you should format some information on its Web pages. Some of the information can be put into lists, such as bulleted or numbered lists. In other cases, when you want to show text side by side with photos of the resort, you realize that lists won't do. In such situations, you've heard that tables can be used to arrange elements on the Web page. You're a little worried that it might be difficult, but your coworker reassures you that with Microsoft FrontPage 2000, it's going to be a snap.

In this lesson, you will learn how to create and format bulleted and numbered lists. You will then learn how to create tables on Web pages, insert text in table cells, format cell text, change the size of rows and columns, and make table borders invisible. Finally, you will learn how to change Web page properties.

Import the Lesson 5 practice Web

In this exercise, you create a new Web based on the files in the Lesson05 folder in the FrontPage 2000 SBS Practice folder. You will use this Web for all the exercises in Lesson 5.

1 On the File menu, point to New, and then click Web.

FrontPage displays the New dialog box.

If your hard disk has a drive letter other than C, substitute the appropriate drive letter in step 2.

2 Click the Import Web Wizard icon. In the Specify The Location Of The New Web text box, delete the default text and type **C:\My Webs\Lesson05**, and then click OK.

FrontPage displays the first Import Web Wizard dialog box.

3 Click the From A Source Directory Of Files option, click the Include Subfolders check box, and click the Browse button.

4 Browse to the Lesson05 folder in the FrontPage 2000 SBS Practice folder, and click OK.

5 Click Next twice, and then click Finish.

FrontPage creates a new Web based on the practice files and places it in the Lesson05 folder.

Creating Lists

If the filename is too long to be completely visible in the Folder List, hold the mouse pointer over the filename for a moment. A ScreenTip will display the complete filename.

You've heard that FrontPage makes it easy to create and format lists. You decide to start by creating two list pages: one with a bulleted list of special programs for kids, and the other with a numbered list of directions to the resort.

Create a bulleted list

In this exercise, you create a bulleted list that describes hotel services and activities for kids.

If you are not working through this lesson sequentially, follow the steps in "Import the Lesson 5 Practice Web" earlier in this lesson.

1 In the Folder List, double-click the file Special_programs_for_kids01.htm.

FrontPage opens the Web page in Page view.

2 Click the line below the heading, and click the Bullets button on the toolbar.

FrontPage inserts a bullet.

3 Type **State-certified daycare for toddlers** and press Enter.

FrontPage creates the first bullet item and moves the insertion point down to the next line, adding a second bullet.

④ Type **Junior lifesaving classes at the pool for ages 12–15** and press Enter.

FrontPage creates the second bullet item and moves the insertion point down to the next line, adding a third bullet.

⑤ Type **Pony rides from 10 A.M. to 3 P.M. every day** and press Enter.

FrontPage creates the last bullet item and moves the insertion point down to the next line, adding a bullet.

Bullets

⑥ On the toolbar, click the Bullets button.

FrontPage removes the bulleted list format from the bottom line.

You can convert existing text to a bulleted list by selecting the text and clicking the Bullets button on the toolbar.

Save

⑦ On the toolbar, click the Save button.

FrontPage saves your changes.

tip

To change a bulleted list to another style of list, right-click one of the bullets, click List Properties, click the Other tab, click the list style you want, and then click OK. You can change the bulleted list to a numbered list, definition list, directory list, or menu list.

Formatting Web Pages

Format a bulleted list

In this exercise, you change the bullet symbol used in a bulleted list.

1 Right-click one of the bullets in the list, and on the shortcut menu, click List Properties.

FrontPage displays the List Properties dialog box. Various bullet styles are displayed.

To quickly change a bulleted list to a numbered list, open the List Properties dialog box, click the Numbers tab, click the numbering style you want, and click OK.

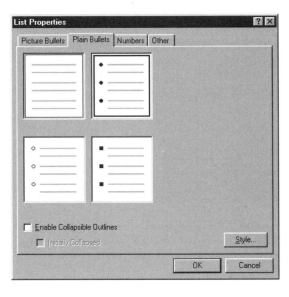

2 Click the lower-right sample box, which displays a square bullet style, and then click OK.

FrontPage changes the bullet style to square bullets.

3 On the toolbar, click the Save button.

FrontPage saves your changes.

Save

tip

To change the style of only one item in a list, right-click the item you want to change, and on the shortcut menu, click List Item Properties. In the dialog box, make the desired changes and click OK.

Create a numbered list

In this exercise, you create a numbered list of driving directions.

Numbering

1 In the Folder List, double-click the file Directions_to_lakewood01.htm.

FrontPage opens the Web page in Page view.

2 Click the line below the heading, and click the Numbering button.

FrontPage inserts the number 1.

3 Type **Take the highway up from Santa Barbara.** and press Enter.

FrontPage moves the insertion point down to the next line, adding the number 2.

You can convert existing text to a numbered list by selecting the text and clicking the Numbering button on the toolbar.

4 Type **Turn left at the scarecrow.** and press Enter.

FrontPage moves the insertion point down to the next line, adding the number 3.

5 Type **Go two miles, and you're here!** and press Enter.

FrontPage moves the insertion point down to the next line, adding the number 4.

Numbering

6 On the toolbar, click the Numbering button.

FrontPage removes the numbered list format from the bottom line.

Save

7 On the toolbar, click the Save button.

FrontPage saves your changes.

---

tip

You can also remove bulleted or numbered list formatting after the last list item by pressing Enter twice or by pressing Enter once and then pressing Backspace.

Format a numbered list

In this exercise, you format the numbers used in a numbered list.

1   Right-click one of the numbers in the list, and on the shortcut menu, click List Properties.

FrontPage displays the List Properties dialog box. Various numbering styles are shown.

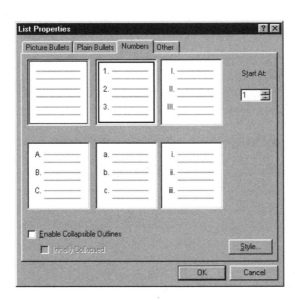

2   Click the lower-right sample box, which displays a lowercase Roman numeral numbering style. Click OK.

FrontPage changes the numbering style to lowercase Roman numerals.

3   On the toolbar, click the Save button.

FrontPage saves your changes.

Save

> **tip**
> To change a numbered list to another style of list, right-click one of the numbers, click List Properties, click the Other tab, click the list style you want, and then click OK. You can change the numbered list to a bulleted list, definition list, directory list, or menu list.

Using Tables to Arrange Page Elements

Many Web pages present data in single-column format. They have text or graphic elements left-aligned, right-aligned, or centered, but Web page elements are still displayed one after another down the page—not side by side. To display a photo and explanatory text side by side, you can use tables.

In addition to their more conventional use of presenting information in a row and column format, tables let you position elements side-by-side on a Web page. You've planned several pages in the Lakewood Mountains Resort Web site that would benefit from using tables. You decide to experiment by creating and formatting a table.

Insert a table

If you are not working through this lesson sequentially, follow the steps in "Import the Lesson 5 Practice Web" earlier in this lesson.

For a demonstration of how to insert a table on a Web page, in the Multimedia folder on the Microsoft FrontPage 2000 Step by Step CD-ROM, double-click the Table icon.

In this exercise, you insert a table on a Web page and specify the table size.

① In the Folder List, double-click the file On_the_town01.htm.

FrontPage displays the Web page in Page view.

② Click the line below the explanatory paragraph. On the Table menu, point to Insert, and then click Table.

FrontPage displays the Insert Table dialog box. The insertion point is in the Rows text box.

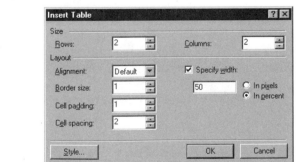

(margin tab) Formatting Web Pages · 5

In the Rows text box, delete the default value of 2, type **3**, and in the Specify Width text box type **100**, and then click OK.

FrontPage inserts a table with three rows and two columns.

Save

 On the toolbar, click the Save button.

FrontPage saves your changes.

Insert Table

tip

Another way to create a table is to click the Insert Table button on the toolbar and drag to select the desired number of rows and columns.

Insert and format text in a table cell

In this exercise, you insert text into a table cell and format the cell contents by changing text alignment and font attributes.

 Click in the top-right table cell, and then type **Visit the original Erewhon power plant, which generated electricity for miners during the California gold rush.**

FrontPage inserts the text into the table cell.

② Press the Tab key twice, and then type **Visit the Erewhon harbor, where fishing boats go out to sea.**

FrontPage moves the insertion point and inserts the text into the cell.

③ Select the two cells containing text.

To move the insertion point to the right and down in a table, press Tab. To move the insertion point to the left and up in a table, press Shift+Tab.

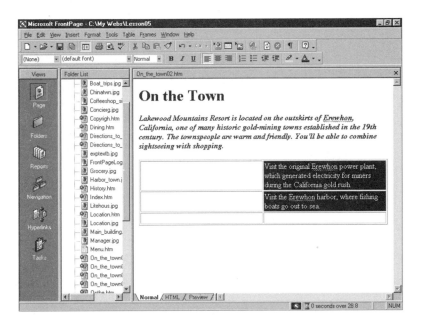

④ Right-click the selected area, and on the shortcut menu, click Cell Properties.

FrontPage displays the Cell Properties dialog box.

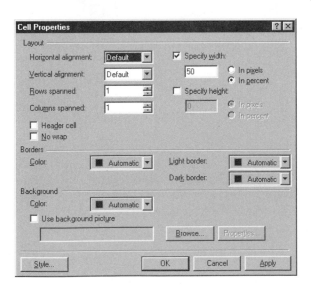

5 Click the Horizontal Alignment drop-down arrow, click Right, and click OK.

The text is right-aligned within the cell.

6 Right-click the selected area again, and on the shortcut menu, click Font.

FrontPage displays the Font dialog box.

7 Click Arial in the Font list, click Bold Italic in the Font Style list, and click OK.

FrontPage changes the font and style of the text in the selected cells.

8 On the toolbar, click the Save button.

FrontPage saves your changes.

Save

Format a table

In this exercise, you format a table by changing its column width, row height, and border style.

1 Position the mouse pointer over the horizontal border below the text *California gold rush*.

*Vertical
Double Arrow*

The mouse pointer changes to a vertical double arrow.

2 Drag the border down approximately ½ inch.

FrontPage makes the row taller and vertically centers the text.

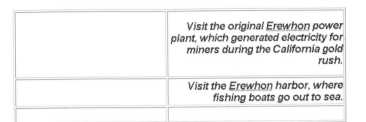

↔

Horizontal Double Arrow

3 Position the mouse pointer over the vertical border in the center of the table.

The mouse pointer changes to a horizontal double arrow.

4 Drag the border approximately ¼ inch to the left.

FrontPage resizes the table columns.

5 Right-click one of the table borders, and on the shortcut menu, click Table Properties.

FrontPage displays the Table Properties dialog box.

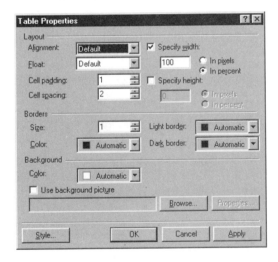

6 Click in the Borders Size text box, delete the default value of 1, and type **0**. Click OK.

FrontPage makes the table borders invisible.

Save

You will learn how to insert images in table cells in Lesson 6, "Adding Multimedia to Web Pages."

7 On the toolbar, click the Save button.

FrontPage saves your changes.

8 In the Folder List, double-click the file On_the_town04.htm.

FrontPage displays a completed version of the table in Page view.

One
Step
Further **Understanding Page Properties**

In the section "Changing Web Page Properties" in Lesson 2, you learned how to use the Page Properties dialog box to change the title of a Web page. Now that you've begun formatting Web pages, your coworker informs you that Web page properties include more than just the titles of your pages. In fact, you can use the following page properties to control the appearance of your Web pages.

- Background pictures and colors.
- Margin widths and heights.
- Hyperlink colors.

Change Web page properties

If you are not working through this lesson sequentially, follow the steps in "Import the Lesson 5 Practice Web" earlier in this lesson.

In this exercise, you add a background picture to a Web page and change the layout of the page.

1 In the Folder List, double-click the file Special_programs_for_kids03.htm.

FrontPage displays the Web page in Page view.

2 Right-click a blank area of the Web page, and on the shortcut menu, click Page Properties.

FrontPage displays the Page Properties dialog box.

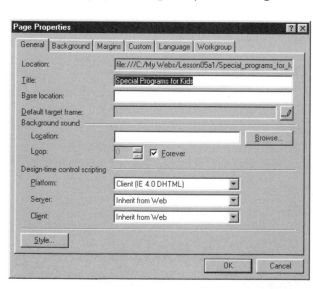

③ Click the Background tab.

④ Click the Background Picture check box and click Browse.

FrontPage displays the Select Background Picture dialog box.

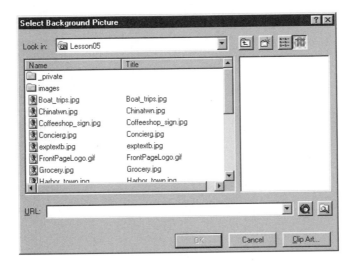

You can use any image file as a background picture. It need not be in the same folder as your Web, and it need not be an image that came with FrontPage.

⑤ In the file list, click the file Exptextb.jpg and click OK.

FrontPage selects the image file as the Web page's background picture.

⑥ Click the Margins tab.

FrontPage displays the Margins section of the dialog box.

⑦ Click the Specify Left Margin check box, type **40** in the Specify Left Margin text box, and click OK.

FrontPage adds a background image to the Web page and moves the page text 40 pixels to the right.

⑧ On the toolbar, click the Save button.

FrontPage saves your changes.

Save

tip

To copy a background from another Web page to the current page, right-click the current page in Page view, click Page Properties, click the Background tab, and click the Get Background Information From Another Page check box. Click Browse, browse to the location of the file that contains the background you want to copy, and then click OK twice.

Formatting Web Pages

Finish the lesson

❶ On the File menu, click Close Web.

❷ For each page, if FrontPage prompts you to save changes, click Yes. FrontPage saves your changes and closes the Lesson05 Web.

Lesson 5 Quick Reference

To	Do this	Button
Create a bulleted list	Click the page location where you want to start the list. On the toolbar, click the Bullets button, and type the list items, pressing Enter after each item.	▤
Format bullets in a bulleted list	Right-click one of the bullets, click List Properties on the shortcut menu, choose a style, and click OK.	
Convert existing text to a bulleted list	Select the text and click the Bullets button on the toolbar.	▤
Create a numbered list	Click the page location where you want to start the list. On the toolbar, click the Numbering button, and type the list items, pressing Enter after each item.	▤
Format numbers in a numbered list	Right-click one of the numbers, click List Properties on the shortcut menu, choose a style, and click OK.	
Change the starting number of a list	Right-click one of the numbers, click List Properties, type the desired number in the Start At text box, and click OK.	
Convert existing text to a numbered list	Select the text and click the Numbering button on the toolbar.	▤
Insert a table	Click the desired page location. On the Table menu, point to Insert, click Table, enter the number of rows and columns, and click OK.	
Insert text in a table cell	Click in the cell, and then type the desired text.	

Lesson 5 Quick Reference

To	Do this
Format text in one or more table cells	Select the text in the cell(s), right-click the selected text, click Cell Properties, Font, or Paragraph, make the changes, and click OK.
Resize a table row or column	Drag a border of the row or column to the appropriate location, and then release the mouse button.
Change a table's border	Right-click a border, click Table Properties on the shortcut menu, make the desired changes, and click OK.
Change Web page properties	Right-click a blank area of the page, click Page Properties, make the changes, and click OK.

6

Adding Multimedia to Web Pages

ESTIMATED TIME 30 min.

In this lesson you will learn how to:

✔ *Insert photos and clip art on a Web page.*

✔ *Create thumbnails of Web page images.*

✔ *Edit Web page images.*

✔ *Add a background sound to a Web page.*

✔ *Add a motion clip to a Web page.*

✔ *Create hover buttons on a Web page.*

So far, the managers of Lakewood Mountains Resort have been very happy with your work on the resort's Web site. However, you'd like to impress them even more by incorporating pictures, sounds, and motion clips on their Web pages. After all, the Web is a graphically oriented way to send information over the Internet. A state-of-the-art Web site should make use of that feature.

Your coworker tells you that Microsoft FrontPage 2000 makes it simple to put all kinds of multimedia on Web pages, so you decide to give it a try. In this lesson, you will learn how to insert photos and clip art images on Web pages, insert images in table cells on a Web page, and create thumbnails. You will also learn how to add a background sound to a Web page and insert a motion clip on a Web page. Finally, you will learn how to create *hover buttons* that change in appearance when a mouse pointer is positioned over them.

Import the Lesson 6 practice Web

In this exercise, you create a new Web based on the files in the Lesson06 folder in the FrontPage 2000 SBS Practice folder. You will use this Web for all the exercises in Lesson 6.

1 On the File menu, point to New, and then click Web.

FrontPage displays the New dialog box.

If your hard disk drive has a letter other than C, substitute the appropriate drive letter in step 2.

2 Click the Import Web Wizard icon. In the Specify The Location Of The New Web text box, type **C:\My Webs\Lesson06**, and then click OK.

FrontPage displays the first Import Web Wizard dialog box.

3 Click the From A Source Directory Of Files option, click the Include Subfolders check box, and click the Browse button.

4 Browse to the Lesson06 folder in the FrontPage 2000 SBS Practice folder, and click OK.

5 Click Next twice, and then click Finish.

FrontPage creates a new Web based on the practice files and places it in the Lesson06 folder.

Using Images on Web Pages

Your first task is to learn how to insert different kinds of images on Web pages. There are essentially two kinds of static images you'll use on Web pages: photo files and clip art. Photo files come in many different file formats, but they're usually either GIF (Graphics Interchange Format) files or JPEG (Joint Photographic Experts Group) files. GIF and JPEG files compress the image, allowing a smaller file size than other formats. This allows GIF and JPEG files to download faster to a Web site visitor's computer.

Likewise, clip art images come in a variety of formats, including GIF, JPEG, BMP (Windows bitmap), and PNG (Portable Network Graphics). However, GIF and JPEG are still the most common formats for clip art files. FrontPage includes an extensive Clip Art Gallery with hundreds of ready-to-use images, including buttons, cartoons, pictures, backgrounds, and many other images. The Clip Art Gallery even includes sound and motion clip files.

Regardless of the file format, you insert photo and clip art images on a Web page in much the same way. In FrontPage, it's just a matter of making a few menu selections. An especially valuable FrontPage feature creates *thumbnails*, which are small versions of images that download very quickly. To create a thumbnail, you first insert a full-sized image file on a Web page. Then you select the image and click the Auto Thumbnail button on the Image toolbar.

On the Web page, FrontPage replaces the original full-sized image with a thumbnail version. By clicking the thumbnail, a Web site visitor can display the full-sized image.

Insert a photo on a Web page

If you are not working through this lesson sequentially, follow the steps in "Import the Lesson 6 Practice Web" earlier in this lesson.

In this exercise, you insert a photo on the Lakewood Mountains Resort Welcome page.

1 In the Folder List, double-click the file Welcome01.htm.

FrontPage displays the Lakewood Welcome page in Page view.

2 Click the blank line underneath the text *Lakewood Mountains Resort* and above the resort's address.

The insertion point is centered on the line.

3 On the Insert menu, point to Picture, and then click From File.

FrontPage displays the Picture dialog box.

4 In the file list, click Main_building.jpg.

FrontPage displays a preview of the image in the preview pane.

For a demonstration of how to insert a photo on a Web page, in the Multimedia folder on the FrontPage 2000 Step by Step CD-ROM, double-click the InsertPhoto icon.

5 Click OK.

FrontPage inserts the image at the location you selected.

6 On the toolbar, click the Save button.

FrontPage saves your changes.

Save

tip

By reducing the size of image files, you reduce the time it takes to download them to the Web site visitor's computer. Apart from reducing the size of the image itself, a good way to shrink file size is to use an image-editing program such as Paint Shop Pro or Microsoft PhotoDraw to reduce the number of colors in the image.

Explore the Clip Art Gallery

In this exercise, you explore the FrontPage Clip Art Gallery.

1 In the Folder List, double-click the file Sights01.htm.

FrontPage displays the Web page.

2 On the Insert menu, point to Picture, and then click Clip Art.

FrontPage displays the Clip Art Gallery window. On the Pictures tab, you can select clip art to insert on Web pages.

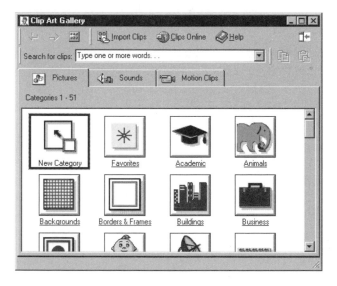

3 Click the Sounds tab.

On the Sounds tab, you can select sound effects to insert on Web pages.

4 Click the Motion Clips tab.

On the Motion Clips tab, you can select motion clips and animated GIF files to insert on Web pages.

⑤ In the Categories pane, click the Academic icon.

FrontPage displays the motion clips available in this category.

If there are no motion clips displayed, you can download clips from the Microsoft Clip Gallery Live.

⑥ Click one of the motion clip pictures.

FrontPage displays the pop-up menu for the motion clip. The clip is an animated GIF file.

An animated GIF file contains a short sequence of images. When a Web site visitor views the GIF file, the images are displayed in rapid sequence, producing an animated picture.

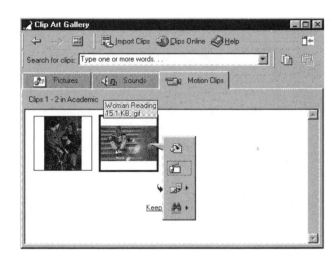

Play Clip

⑦ On the pop-up menu, click the Play Clip button.

FrontPage plays the motion clip in the GIF Player window.

⑧ Click the Close button at the top-right corner of the GIF Player window.

FrontPage closes the GIF Player window.

Back
The Forward and Back buttons work just as they do in Microsoft Internet Explorer.

⑨ On the Clip Art Gallery toolbar, click the Back button.

FrontPage redisplays the Motion Clips tab of the Clip Art Gallery window.

⑩ Click the Close button at the top-right corner of the Clip Art Gallery window.

FrontPage closes the window.

tip

To download additional clip art, sounds, and motion clips from the Web, connect to the Internet, and click the Clips Online button on the toolbar in the Clip Art Gallery window. FrontPage connects to the Microsoft Clip Gallery Live site on the World Wide Web, from which you can download additional clip art images for your Web pages. You can also download clip art, sounds, and motion clip files from newsgroups on the Internet, such as *alt.binaries.sounds.midi*.

Search the Clip Art Gallery

In this exercise, you search for clip art in the Clip Art Gallery.

1 On the Sights01 Web page, click the blank line below the heading and above the table.

FrontPage moves the insertion point to the line below the heading.

2 On the Insert menu, point to Picture, and then click Clip Art.

FrontPage displays the Clip Art Gallery window.

3 Click in the Search For Clips text box, type **arrow**, and then press Enter.

FrontPage searches the Clip Art Gallery for arrow images and displays the search results on the Pictures tab.

The window on your screen might differ slightly from the one shown in the illustration.

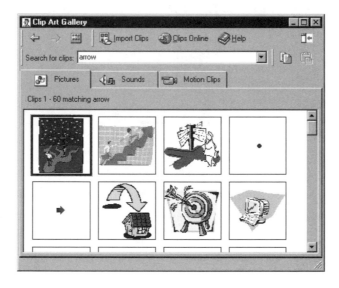

Insert clip art on a Web page

If your window does not contain the globe-arrow image, just use any clip art image you like.

In this exercise, you select a clip art image, insert it on a Web page, and then save the Web page.

1 Click the globe-arrow image.

FrontPage displays the pop-up menu for the clip art image.

2 On the pop-up menu, click the Insert Clip button.

FrontPage inserts the globe-arrow clip art at the selected location on the Web page and closes the Clip Art Gallery window.

Insert Clip

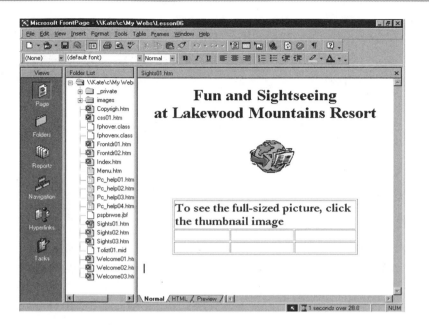

Save

③ On the toolbar, click the Save button, and then click OK in the Save Embedded Files dialog box.

FrontPage saves the Web page with your changes.

tip
You can make almost any image on a Web page a hyperlink, including clip art. To make a clip art image a hyperlink, right-click the image, and click Hyperlink on the shortcut menu. In the Create Hyperlink dialog box, browse to the file that will be the link target, click the file, and click OK.

Insert images in table cells and create thumbnails

In this exercise, you arrange images on a Web page by inserting them in table cells. You then shrink the images by converting them to thumbnails that link to the full-sized images.

① In the Folder List, double-click the file Sights02.htm.

FrontPage opens the Web page in Page view.

② Click in the top-left cell of the first empty row in the table. On the Insert menu, point to Picture, and click From File.

FrontPage displays the Picture dialog box.

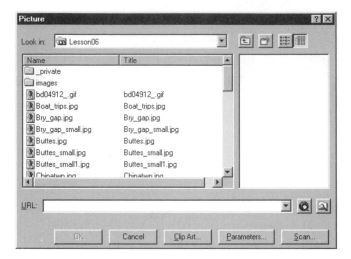

3 In the file list, click Bry_gap.jpg, and then click OK.

FrontPage inserts the image into the table cell. Notice that the image is too large to fit in the table cell.

4 Click the image in the table cell.

FrontPage displays the Image toolbar along the bottom of your screen.

Auto Thumbnail

5 On the Image toolbar, click the Auto Thumbnail button.

FrontPage converts the table image into a much smaller thumbnail that contains a hyperlink to the full-sized image.

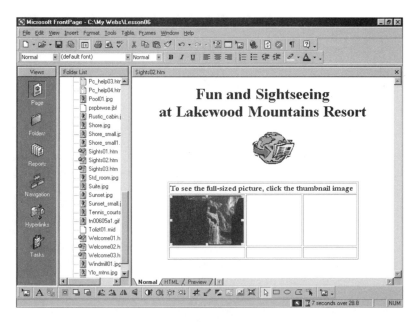

6 Click in the middle cell of the same row. On the Insert menu, point to Picture, click From File, click Shore.jpg, and then click OK.

FrontPage inserts an image into the middle cell of the row.

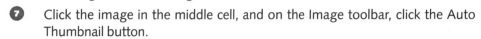

Auto Thumbnail

7 Click the image in the middle cell, and on the Image toolbar, click the Auto Thumbnail button.

FrontPage creates a thumbnail image and links it to the full-sized image.

Save

8 On the toolbar, click the Save button, and click OK in the Save Embedded Files dialog box.

FrontPage saves your changes.

Move image files to the images folder

When you create a Web, FrontPage automatically includes an images folder. If your Web has a large number of images, moving all image files to the images folder makes your Web easier to manage. In this exercise, you move image files from your Web's main folder to its images folder and observe how FrontPage updates the images' hyperlinks.

1 On the Views bar, click the Folders icon.

FrontPage displays a list of all files and folders in the Lesson06 Web.

2 Click the Type button at the top of the file list.

FrontPage displays the files in alphabetical order by type.

If files are displayed in reverse order, click the Type button one more time.

3 In the file list, click Boat_trips.jpg. Scroll down until you see Ylo_mtns_small.jpg, hold down Shift, and click that file.

4 Drag the selected files to the images subfolder in the Folder List.

FrontPage moves all the JPEG image files to the images subfolder and updates all hyperlinks between Web pages and JPEG files to reflect the files' new location.

5 In the file list, click FrontPageLogo.gif, hold down the Ctrl key, and click any other GIF files.

The GIF image files are selected.

The Sights03.htm page is a completed version of the Sights01.htm page that you worked on earlier.

6 Drag the GIF image files to the images subfolder.

FrontPage moves all the GIF image files to the images subfolder and updates the hyperlinks.

7 On the Views bar, click the Page icon, and then double-click Sights03.htm in the Folder List.

FrontPage displays the Web page in Page view.

8   Right-click the picture in the top-left table cell, and then on the shortcut menu, click Hyperlink Properties.

FrontPage displays the Edit Hyperlink dialog box. Notice that the hyperlink's target (in the URL text box) has been updated and is in the images folder.

9   Click the Cancel button in the Edit Hyperlinks dialog box.

FrontPage closes the Edit Hyperlinks dialog box.

Editing Images on Web Pages

Placing an image on a Web page is easy, but often the image is too large or too small to fit properly on the Web page. Moreover, some Web site visitors set up their Web browsers to download Web pages without embedded images: this makes the pages download more quickly, but leaves gaps where images would otherwise appear. FrontPage enables you to specify "alternative text" that is displayed when images aren't downloaded. Instead of the image, visitors see your alternative text description at the page location where the image would have appeared.

Resize an image

If you are not working through this lesson sequentially, follow the steps in "Import the Lesson 6 Practice Web" earlier in this lesson.

In this exercise, you resize an image on a Web page.

1   In the Folder List, double-click Welcome02.htm.

FrontPage displays the Welcome02.htm Web page in Page view. The hotel image is so large that it pushes the address and phone number off the bottom of the screen.

2   Click the hotel image, and then scroll to the lower-right corner of the image.

A small square (a resize handle) appears at the corner of the image.

3   Move the mouse pointer over the resize handle.

The mouse pointer changes into a diagonal double arrow.

Double Arrow

4   Drag the mouse pointer upward and to the left to shrink the image.

FrontPage resizes the hotel image, retaining the original proportions, as shown in the illustration on the following page.

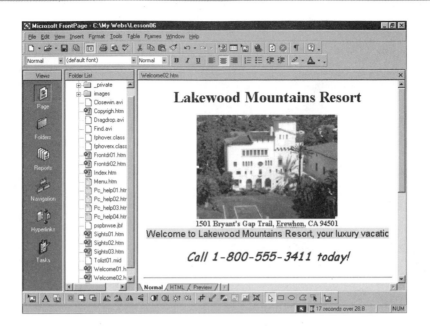

Specify alternative text for an image

In this exercise, you specify alternative text for an image on a Web page.

➊ Right-click the hotel image, and then on the shortcut menu, click Picture Properties.

FrontPage displays the Picture Properties dialog box.

2 Click in the Text text box under Alternative Representations, type **Lakewood Mountains Resort main building**, and click OK.

FrontPage inserts the text to be displayed if a Web site visitor's browser does not display Web page images.

3 On the toolbar, click the Save button.

FrontPage saves your changes.

Save

Adding Sound Effects and Music to Web Pages

Most Web page content is informative, but there's more to the Web surfing experience than just getting information. You want the Lakewood Mountains Resort Web site to be a pleasant place to visit. One way to make the site interesting is to add a background sound to the home page. This background sound will play as long as the home page is displayed in a Web browser.

important

When you use these steps to insert a sound file on a Web page, the sound file will play only if the page is loaded in Microsoft's Internet Explorer Web browser—but not if the user loads it into Netscape's Navigator Web browser. Netscape Navigator uses different HTML coding to play a background sound.

Add a background sound

If you are not working through this lesson sequentially, follow the steps in "Import the Lesson 6 Practice Web" earlier in the lesson.

In this exercise, you add a background sound to a Web page and preview the sound in your Web browser.

1 In the Folder List, double-click Welcome03.htm.

FrontPage displays the Welcome03.htm Web page in Page view.

2 Right-click a blank area of the page, and then click Page Properties.

FrontPage displays the Page Properties dialog box.

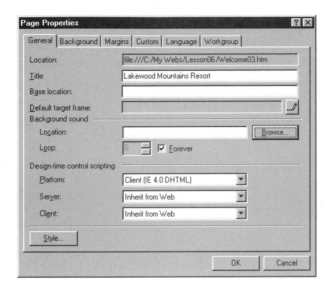

③ Click the Browse button.

FrontPage displays the Background Sound dialog box.

④ Click Tolizt01.mid, and click OK twice.

FrontPage inserts the file as a background sound that will play as long as the page is displayed in a visitor's Web browser.

Save

⑤ On the toolbar, click the Save button, and then click the Preview In Browser button.

FrontPage saves the page and displays it in your Web browser. If you are using Microsoft Internet Explorer, the background sound plays automatically.

Preview in Browser

⑥ Click the Close button at the top-right corner of your Web browser window.

Your Web browser closes and FrontPage reappears.

Close

tip

By default, a background sound continues to play as long as the Web page is displayed in a visitor's Web browser. However, you can specify that the sound play a certain number of times and then stop. In the Page Properties dialog box, clear the Forever check box. In the Loop text box, enter the number of times the background sound should repeat, and then click OK.

Adding Video to Web Pages

So far, you've had great success using FrontPage to insert static pictures on Web pages. What's even more impressive, however, is that you can just as easily insert motion clips on Web pages. When Web site visitors load a page with an embedded motion clip, the video will automatically play both motion and sound. You can also create hyperlinks that lead to motion clip files.

Insert a motion clip

If you are not working through this lesson sequentially, follow the steps in "Import the Lesson 6 Practice Web" earlier in this lesson.

In this exercise, you insert a motion clip on a Web page and preview the video in your Web browser.

❶ In the Folder List, double-click Pc_help01.htm.

FrontPage displays the Web page in Page view.

❷ Click the empty line just below the page text. On the Insert menu, point to Picture, and then click Video.

FrontPage displays the Video dialog box.

The file Pc_help02.htm is the completed version of the page you edit in this exercise.

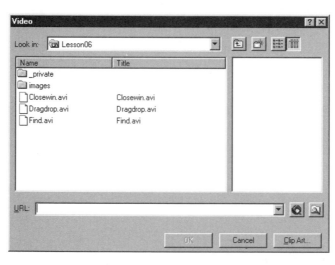

❸ Click Closewin.avi in the Lesson06 folder, and then click OK.

FrontPage inserts the motion clip directly on the Web page. When a Web site visitor displays the page, the video will play once.

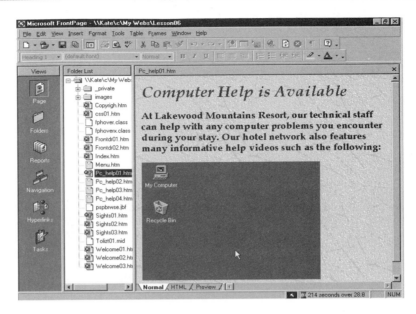

Adding Multimedia

6

Save

*Preview
In Browser*

Close

4. On the toolbar, click the Save button, and then click the Preview In Browser button.

   FrontPage saves the page and displays it in your Web browser. The motion clip plays automatically.

5. Click the Close button at the top-right corner of your Web browser window.

   Your Web browser closes and FrontPage reappears.

Link to a motion clip

In this exercise, you create a hyperlink to a motion clip file instead of inserting the file directly on a Web page.

1. In the Folder List, double-click Pc_help03.htm.

   FrontPage displays the Web page in Page view.

2. Select the text *How to drag and drop*.

3. Right-click the selected text, and on the shortcut menu, click Hyperlink.

   FrontPage displays the Create Hyperlink dialog box.

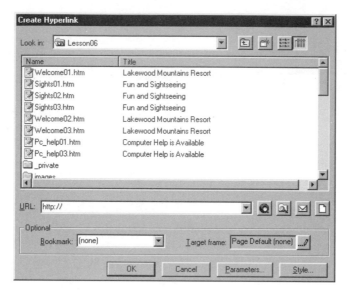

The file Pc_help04.htm is the completed version of the page you edit in this exercise.

4 In the file list, click Dragdrop.avi, and then click OK.

FrontPage inserts the hyperlink.

Save

5 On the toolbar, click the Save button, and then click the Preview In Browser button.

FrontPage saves the Web page and displays it in your Web browser.

Preview In Browser

6 Click the hyperlink How To Drag And Drop.

The Windows Media Player opens and plays the motion clip.

Close

7. Close the Media Player and your Web browser.

   FrontPage is redisplayed.

Using Style Sheets to Position Web Page Items

New! 2000

One of the exciting but somewhat advanced techniques supported by FrontPage 2000 is the ability to use Web page *style sheets* to control the appearance of your Web pages. A Web page style sheet is a separate text file in which you specify how various elements of your Web page should look. Techniques for creating style sheets—called *cascading style sheets* (CSS) because you can apply multiple style sheets to a single Web page—are defined by the World Wide Web Consortium (*www.w3.org*).

FrontPage makes it easy to use one of the most powerful style sheet features to be added in the latest CSS version: absolute and relative positioning of Web page elements. Previously, you've seen how you can use tables to place items in specific locations on your Web pages. That's how it's been done for most of the Web's history. With style sheets, however, you can position Web page items exactly where you want them *without* using tables.

With FrontPage, you don't have to write any style sheet code to position Web page items. You simply use menu choices and dialog boxes to specify the position you want for an item. FrontPage does all the work of creating the style sheet code; you never even have to see it.

Use a style sheet to position an image

If you are not working through this lesson sequentially, follow the steps in "Import the Lesson 6 Practice Web" earlier in this lesson.

1. On the Views bar, click the Page icon.

   FrontPage displays the Web in Page view.

2. On the toolbar, click the New button.

   FrontPage creates a new Web page and displays it in Page view.

3. On the Insert menu, point to Picture, and then click From File.

   FrontPage displays the Picture dialog box.

New

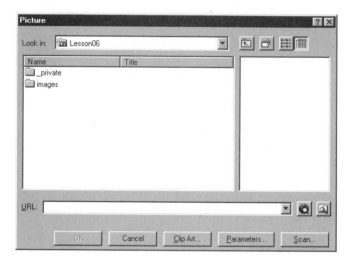

4 Double-click the Images folder, click Bry_gap_small.jpg, and click OK.

FrontPage inserts the picture at the top-left corner of the Web page.

5 On the Insert menu, point to Picture, and then click From File.

FrontPage displays the Picture dialog box.

6 In the dialog box's file list, click Shore_small.jpg, and click OK.

FrontPage inserts the new picture just to the right of the first picture.

7 Right-click the second picture (Shore_small.jpg). On the shortcut menu, click Picture Properties. Click the Style button, click the Format button, and in the drop-down menu, click Position.

FrontPage displays the Position dialog box.

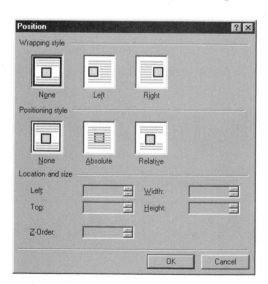

8 In the Positioning Style section of the dialog box, click the Absolute icon. Type **300** in the Left text box and type **50** in the Top text box.

FrontPage will position the picture 300 pixels from the left edge of the Web page and 50 pixels from the top of the Web page.

9 Click OK three times.

FrontPage closes all the dialog boxes and positions the picture at the location you specified.

10 Right-click the first picture (Bry_gap_small.jpg). On the shortcut menu, click Picture Properties. Click the Style button, click the Format button, and in the drop-down menu, click Position.

FrontPage displays the Position dialog box.

11 In the Positioning Style section, click the Absolute icon. Type **50** in the Left text box and type **50** in the Top text box.

FrontPage will position the picture 50 pixels from the left edge of the Web page and 50 pixels from the top of the Web page.

12 Click OK three times.

FrontPage closes all the dialog boxes and positions the picture at the location you specified.

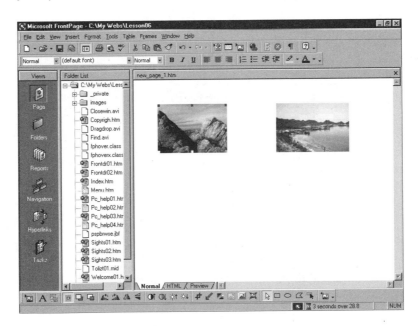

Save

13 On the toolbar, click the Save button, type **CSS01.htm** in the File Name text box, and click Save.

FrontPage saves your changes.

> **tip**
> You can use style sheets to position items on a Web page with *absolute* or *relative* positioning. Absolute positioning, which you used in the previous exercise, places the item at exactly the distance you specify from the top and left edges of the page—even if there's another item in that location. Relative positioning moves the item the specified distance down and to the right from the point at which it would normally appear, not from the edges of the page. Thus, relative positioning is slightly safer but doesn't give you as much control.

One Step Further   Creating Hover Buttons

Motion clips aren't the only kind of animation you can create with FrontPage. Another popular multimedia effect is the *hover button*, whose appearance changes if a Web site visitor points to it with the mouse—that is, when the mouse pointer "hovers" over the button.

A hover button is actually a Java applet created by FrontPage. You can use a hover button to link to another Web page. When a Web site visitor points to the hover button, the button displays a hover effect such as changing color or appearing to have been pushed. When a Web site visitor clicks the hover button, the linked Web page is displayed.

Create a hover button

If you are not working through this lesson sequentially, follow the steps in "Import the Lesson 6 Practice Web" earlier in this lesson.

In this exercise, you create a hover button and set its properties.

1 In the Folder List, double-click Frontdr01.htm.

FrontPage opens the Web page and displays it in Page view.

2 Click the line below the *Welcome* text. On the Insert menu, point to Component, and then click Hover Button.

FrontPage displays the Hover Button Properties dialog box. The default text in the Button Text box is already selected.

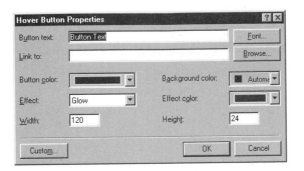

The file Frontdr02.htm is a completed version of the file you edit in this exercise.

3 Type **Enter the Web Site** in the Button Text text box. Type **300** in the Width text box and **50** in the Height text box.

FrontPage sets the button caption and size.

4 Click the Effect drop-down arrow.

FrontPage displays a list of animation effects you can use with hover buttons.

5 Click Bevel In.

FrontPage sets the button to look as if it has been pressed when the mouse pointer is on it.

6 Click the Browse button.

FrontPage displays the Select Hover Button Hyperlink dialog box.

7 Scroll down in the file list, click Index.htm, and click OK twice.

FrontPage creates a hover button with the properties you specified.

Save

8 On the toolbar, click the Save button, and then click the Preview In Browser button.

FrontPage saves your changes and displays the page in your Web browser.

*Preview
In Browser*

9 Move the mouse pointer over the hover button.

The hover button text moves slightly, as if the button has been pressed inward.

10 Click the hover button.

Your Web browser loads the Web's home page.

tip
Another way to create a hyperlink hover button is to right-click the button and click Hover Button Properties on the shortcut menu. The Hover Button dialog box will be displayed. In the Link To text box, browse to the file that will be the link target, click the file, and click OK.

Adding Multimedia

6

Finish the lesson

Close

① Click the Close button at the top-right corner of your Web browser window. Your Web browser closes and FrontPage reappears.

② On the File menu, click Close Web.

③ For each page, if FrontPage prompts you to save changes, click Yes. FrontPage saves your changes and closes the Lesson06 Web.

Lesson 6 Quick Reference

To	Do this	Button
Insert a photo on a Web page	Click the desired location on the Web page. On the Insert menu, point to Picture, and click From File. Browse to the desired file, click it, and click OK.	
Search the Clip Art Gallery	On the Insert menu, point to Picture, and click Clip Art. In the Search For Clips text box, type the search text, and press Enter.	
Insert clip art on a Web page	Click the desired location on the Web page. On the Insert menu, point to Picture, and click Clip Art. Click a category, click the desired clip art, and click the Insert Clip button.	
Insert an image in a table cell	Click in the desired table cell. On the Insert menu, point to Picture, and click From File. In the file list, click the desired image, and click OK.	
Move image files to the images folder	Click the Folders icon on the Views bar, and click the Type button at the top of the file list. Select the image files, and drag them to the images folder in the Folder List.	
Create image thumbnails	Click the image on the Web page, and then click the Auto Thumbnail button on the Image toolbar.	

Lesson 6 Quick Reference

To	Do this
Resize an image	Click the image to select it, and then drag one of its resize handles to resize the image.
Add a background sound to a Web page	Right-click a blank area of the Web page, and on the shortcut menu, click Page Properties. Click the Browse button, select the desired sound file, and click OK twice.
Specify alternative text for an image	Right-click the image, and on the shortcut menu, click Picture Properties. Click in the Text text box, type the alternative text, and then click OK.
Insert a motion clip directly on a Web page	Click the desired location on the Web page. On the Insert menu, point to Picture, and click Video. Select the desired motion clip, and then click OK.
Link to a motion clip	Select and right-click the text or image for the link. On the shortcut menu, click Hyperlink. Select the desired video file, and then click OK.
Create a hover button	Click the desired location on the Web page. On the Insert menu, point to Component, and click Hover Button. Enter the button text and dimensions, click the Effect drop-down arrow, select an effect from the list box, and click the Browse button. Browse to the file you want the hover button to link to, and click OK twice.

6

Adding Multimedia

2

Review & Practice

**ESTIMATED
TIME
20 min.**

> **You will review and practice how to:**
>
> ✔ *Apply FrontPage themes.*
> ✔ *Use FrontPage components.*
> ✔ *Create numbered and bulleted lists.*
> ✔ *Use tables to arrange Web page elements.*
> ✔ *Insert photos and clip art on Web pages.*
> ✔ *Create thumbnail images.*
> ✔ *Add background sounds to Web pages.*
> ✔ *Insert video clips on Web pages.*

Before you go on to Part 3, which covers creating forms to get user feedback and frames to enhance your Web site, you should review the skills you've learned in Part 2 by working through this Review & Practice section. You will review how to apply Microsoft FrontPage themes, use FrontPage components, create lists, insert tables to arrange page elements, insert photos and clip art, create thumbnail images, add background sounds, and insert video clips.

Scenario

Your coworkers are eager to use FrontPage for their own projects, and they have bombarded you with questions about Web design. One of their most common questions is: "What else can you do with FrontPage?"

To answer that question, you've agreed to demonstrate some intermediate-level FrontPage techniques. You've decided to show how to apply FrontPage themes, use FrontPage components, insert images, and several other skills.

Step 1:   Enhance a Web Page

1 Start FrontPage and use the Personal Web template to create a simple Web.

2 Display the Web in Navigation view and apply the Citrus Punch theme to all pages of the Web. Apply a different theme to only a selected page of the Web.

3 Display the home page in Page view. Replace the final paragraph of the default text with a hit counter. After inserting the hit counter, change its properties by selecting a different counter style, and set the counter to display only seven digits.

4 Save the home page with your changes and close the home page.

For more information about	See
Creating a Web	Lesson 2
Using wizards and templates	Lesson 2
Using FrontPage themes	Lesson 4
Inserting FrontPage components	Lesson 4
Changing component properties	Lesson 4

Step 2:   Format a Web Page

New

1 On the toolbar, click the New button.

2 On the new page, create a numbered list with the following steps:

1. **Create a new page.**
2. **Click the Numbering button on the toolbar.**
3. **Type the list items.**

Numbering

3 Press Enter twice to create a blank line under the numbered list. Create a bulleted list with the following items:

- **Themes**
- **Components**
- **Templates**

Bullets

4 Press Enter twice to create a blank line under the bulleted list. Insert a two-row by two-column table.

5 In the top-left table cell, type **Main Building**. In the top-right table cell, type **Swimming Pool**.

6 Select the two cells in the top row. Change the cell properties to center the cell contents horizontally.

7 Display the Page Properties dialog box and change the page title to Formatting Demonstration. Save the page as Format01.htm.

For more information about	See
Creating a new page	Lesson 2
Saving a page	Lesson 2
Creating a numbered list	Lesson 5
Creating a bulleted list	Lesson 5
Inserting a table	Lesson 5
Changing cell properties	Lesson 5
Changing page properties	Lesson 5

Step 3:   ## Add Images, Sounds, and Video

1   In the lower-left cell, insert the image file Main_building.jpg from the Review02\images folder in the FrontPage 2000 SBS Practice folder.

2   Create a thumbnail image of the building photo. Repeat the process to insert Pool01.jpg in the lower-right cell and create a thumbnail image.

3   From the Review02 folder in the FrontPage 2000 SBS Practice folder, insert the file The Microsoft Sound.wav as a background sound on the page. Set the sound to play only once, when the page is first opened.

4   From the Review02 folder in the FrontPage 2000 SBS Practice folder, insert the video clip Closewin.avi below the table on the page.

5   Delete the video clip from the page, and then replace it with a hyperlink to the video clip.

For more information about	See
Inserting images in table cells	Lesson 6
Creating thumbnail images	Lesson 6
Inserting a background sound	Lesson 6
Inserting a motion clip	Lesson 6
Creating a link to a motion clip	Lesson 6

Finish the Review & Practice

1   Save your changes on the Format01 page.

2   Close the Review02 Web.

PART 3

Advanced Web Site Techniques

7

Creating Forms for User Feedback

In this lesson you will learn how to:

✔ *Use the Form Page Wizard.*

✔ *Create a form from scratch.*

✔ *Add fields and text to forms.*

✔ *Modify form fields.*

✔ *Send form data to a text file or e-mail address.*

✔ *Create a guest book page.*

ESTIMATED
TIME
35 min.

So far, you've created a fairly impressive Web site to showcase the attractions of Lakewood Mountains Resort. But as Web users become more sophisticated, it's not enough merely to present static information on the Web. Web site visitors often want to be able to send information or comments to a Web site and get a reply from the site's owner. The manager of Lakewood Mountains Resort would like you to make it possible for Web site visitors to send their contact information and vacation plans, to reserve a room, or to request more information about the resort.

In this lesson, you will learn how to create Web page forms that let visitors send data to the Web site. You'll also learn how to create forms with the Form Page Wizard; how to create forms "from scratch" on an existing Web page; how to add fields and text to a form; and how to route form data to a Web page, an e-mail address, a database, or a Web server program. Finally, you will learn how to create a guest book page that allows visitors to sign in and leave comments.

Import the Lesson 7 practice Web

In this exercise, you create a new Web based on the files in the Lesson07 folder in the FrontPage 2000 SBS Practice folder. You will use this Web for all the exercises in Lesson 7.

1 On the File menu, point to New, and then click Web.

FrontPage displays the New dialog box.

If your hard disk drive has a drive letter other than C, substitute the appropriate drive letter in step 2.

2 Click the Import Web Wizard icon. In the Specify The Location Of The New Web text box, delete the default text and type **C:\My Webs\Lesson07**, and click OK.

FrontPage displays the first Import Web Wizard dialog box.

3 Click the From A Source Directory Of Files option, click the Include Subfolders check box, and click the Browse button.

4 Browse to the Lesson07 folder in the FrontPage 2000 SBS Practice folder, and click OK.

5 Click Next twice, and then click Finish.

FrontPage creates a new Web based on the practice files and places it in the Lesson07 folder.

Understanding Forms

Forms are everywhere. You fill out a form at the bank to get money from your account, at the Motor Vehicle Department to get your driver's license, and even at some pizza restaurants to place your order. Most paper forms have a common structure: a list of questions accompanied by areas in which you can write your answers. Some forms also include check boxes that let you select from multiple predetermined options. When you've filled out the form, you hand it to the salesperson, bank teller, or clerk, who takes actions based on the information you provided.

Web page forms work in the same way. When Web site visitors load a page containing a form, they can type information into text boxes. They can also click check boxes and radio buttons, make choices from drop-down menus, and type free-form text into scrolling text boxes that can hold more text than they display on the screen. And instead of physically handing a paper form to someone, Web site visitors just click a Submit button to send the form data to the Web server where it can be sent to a file, e-mail address, or a server program for further processing.

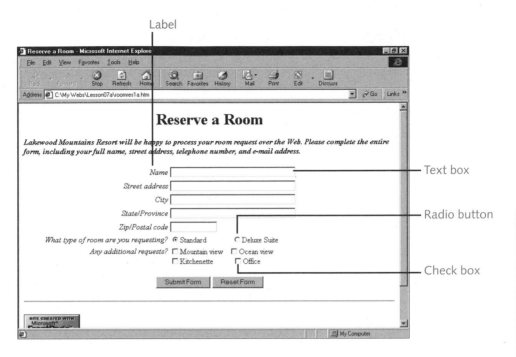

Creating Forms in FrontPage

To create a form without FrontPage, you would need a pretty good understanding of HTML, as well as how to use its various form tags, such as <FORM>, <INPUT>, and so on. With FrontPage, however, you need no HTML knowledge to create a form. All you need is the keyboard or the mouse.

There are three ways to create a form: use the Form Page Wizard, use a form page template, or create your form from scratch. When you create a form with the Form Page Wizard, FrontPage asks you a series of questions about what you want on your form. It creates a form based on your answers. You can then modify the form to fit your exact needs. Using a template is slightly simpler: instead of asking you questions, FrontPage just creates a form based on a particular design—say, for a Guest Book page. Then you can modify the form to suit your particular needs.

When you create a form from scratch, you first create a Web page and then insert a form area on the page. Inside the form border, FrontPage has already inserted a Submit Form button, as well as a Reset Form button. You just insert the text and form fields that you need. You can also create a new form by inserting any form field on the page, outside of any existing forms.

Types of Form Controls

Web page forms use controls that are defined in the HTML language. FrontPage's form controls are summarized in the following table.

Form control	Explanation
Form	Inserts a form area on a Web page.
One-line text box	Inserts a one-line text box on a form (that is, inside the form border on a Web page).
Scrolling text box	Inserts a scrolling text box on a form. Web site visitors can type as much text as they wish.
Check box	Inserts a check box on a form. Visitors can click multiple check boxes to select from pre-defined alternatives.
Radio button	Inserts a radio button (option button) on a form. Visitors can click only one of a group of radio buttons to select from a group of predefined alternatives.
Drop-down menu	Inserts a drop-down menu on a form—similar to a group of radio buttons. Visitors can (by default) click only one of a group of predefined alternatives. Better than radio buttons for presenting a large number of alternatives; also can be set to allow multiple selections.
Push button	Inserts a push button on a form. Visitors click the button to perform an action. Not usually needed because FrontPage automatically creates Submit Form and Reset Form buttons when you create a form. You can insert push buttons to display message boxes, execute Web page scripts, and perform other tasks not directly related to the submission of form data to a server.
Picture	Inserts a picture on a form. You can use a picture in the same way you use a button.
Label	When a form field and its label are both selected, makes the label "clickable" to activate the form field.

Create a form with the Form Page Wizard

If you are not working through this lesson sequentially, follow the steps in "Import the Lesson 7 Practice Web" earlier in the lesson.

In this exercise, you create a form to collect a visitor's contact information using the FrontPage Form Page Wizard.

1 Make sure your Web is displayed in Page view, and then on the File menu, point to New, and click Page.

The New dialog box appears.

2 Click the Form Page Wizard icon, and then click OK.

FrontPage displays the first Form Page Wizard dialog box.

3 Click the Next button.

FrontPage displays the second Form Page Wizard dialog box.

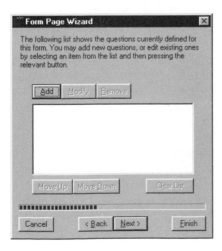

4 Click the Add button to add information to the form.

The dialog box lists the different types of information the wizard can set up the form to collect.

Notice that as you create your form, a progress bar appears at the bottom of the Form Page Wizard dialog box. The progress bar shows how far along you've come in creating your form.

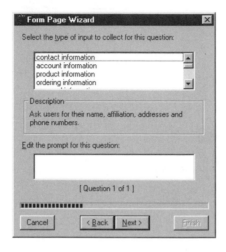

If you accept the default question text, you can always change it later.

5 In the Select The Type Of Input To Collect For This Question box, click Contact Information. In the Edit The Prompt For This Question text box, delete the default text, and then type **Please enter your full name and street address:**. Click the Next button.

The wizard asks what contact information the form should collect.

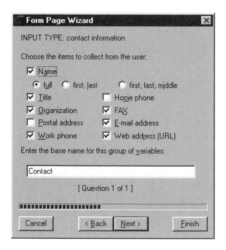

⑥ In the dialog box, clear the check boxes for Title, Organization, Work Phone, Fax, E-mail Address, and Web Address. Click the check boxes for Postal Address and Home Phone, and then click the Next button.

The dialog box displays the list of questions that will appear on the form.

Add radio buttons with the Form Page Wizard

In this exercise, you use the Form Page Wizard to add radio buttons, which will allow visitors to select the type of room they would like.

① In the Form Page Wizard dialog box, click the Add button.

The dialog box lists the different types of information the wizard can set up the form to collect.

② In the Select The Type Of Input To Collect For This Question box, scroll down and click One Of Several Options. Delete the default text in the Edit The Prompt For This Question text box, and then type **What type of room would you like?** and click the Next button.

The wizard displays a dialog box that you can use to create a list of radio buttons.

③ In the Enter The Labels For The Options text box, type the following list, pressing Enter at the end of each line:

Standard Room
Deluxe Suite
Honeymoon Suite

A variable is like a little box in which you can store a value, such as a number or a text string. Later, when needed, your Web site can retrieve the value from the box.

④ Click the Radio Buttons option. In the Enter The Name Of A Variable To Hold This Answer text box, type **roomtype**.

The dialog box should look like the following illustration.

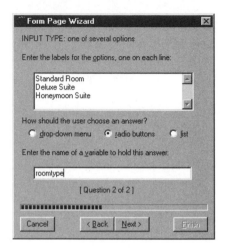

⑤ Click the Next button.

The wizard redisplays the list of questions that will appear on the form.

tip

FrontPage enables you to use exclusive alternatives in three different ways: in a drop-down menu, in a group of radio buttons, or in a list. These three methods all let a Web site visitor select only one of a group of options. The method you choose is a matter of taste. However, if you need to display a large number of options, a drop-down menu is best because it requires little space on the form.

Add check boxes with the Form Page Wizard

In this exercise, you add check boxes (which will allow visitors to select features they would like in their rooms) with the Form Page Wizard.

① In the Form Page Wizard dialog box, click the Add button.

The dialog box lists the different types of information that the wizard can set up the form to collect.

2   In the Select The Type Of Input To Collect For This Question box, scroll down and click Any Of Several Options. Delete the default text in the Edit The Prompt For This Question text box, type **What extra features would you like?**, and click the Next button.

The Form Page Wizard displays a dialog box that you can use to create a list of check boxes.

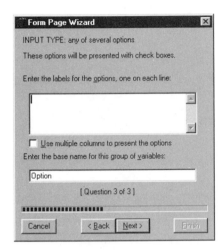

3   In the Enter The Labels For The Options text box, type the following list, pressing Enter at the end of each line:

Kitchenette

Office

Internet Connection

4   Click the Use Multiple Columns To Present The Options check box. In the Enter The Base Name For This Group Of Variables text box, delete the default text, and type **extras**

The dialog box should look like the illustration on the following page.

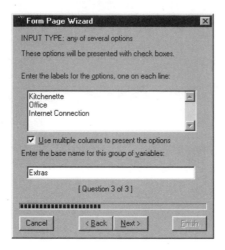

5 Click the Next button.

The wizard redisplays the list of questions that will appear on the form.

Choosing Between Radio Buttons and Check Boxes

Radio buttons and check boxes look similar, but they differ in a vital way. Radio buttons are used to present a group of mutually exclusive alternatives; the Web site visitor is allowed to select only one of the alternatives. For example, if you want a visitor to specify what day of the week he or she will arrive at the resort, the visitor must specify only one day. Check boxes present a set of choices; the visitor can select one or more of them. If you want a Web site visitor to specify his or her favorite recreational activities, multiple selections should be allowed: liking tennis doesn't exclude liking swimming, boating, or bungee jumping.

Finish creating a form with the Form Page Wizard

In this exercise, you title and save a form.

1 In the Form Page Wizard dialog box, click the Finish button.

The Form Page Wizard creates a form based on your input.

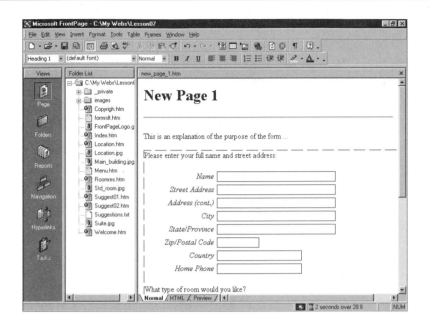

The dotted line on the Web page shows the form border. Anything inside the border is on the form; anything outside the border is not. Although it's unusual, you can have more than one form on the same Web page.

② On the File menu, click Save As.

FrontPage displays the Save As dialog box.

③ In the File Name text box, type **Roomres01.htm**.

④ Click the Change button.

FrontPage displays the Set Page Title dialog box.

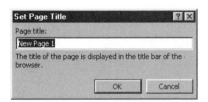

⑤ In the Page Title text box, type **Room Request Form**, click OK, and click the Save button.

FrontPage saves the form page.

⑥ Scroll down to view the bottom part of the form, and then scroll back to the top of the form.

The Form Page Wizard created radio buttons and check boxes as you instructed. At the bottom of the page, the wizard inserted a Submit Form button and a Reset Form button.

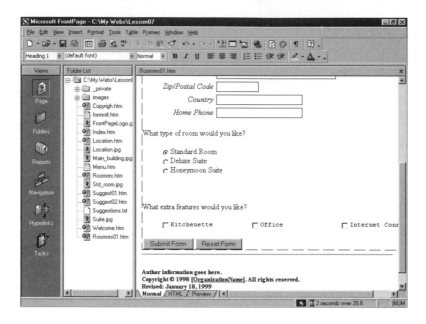

Edit form text

If you insert a Page Banner component on a page, the page title is displayed in the banner at the top of the page.

In this exercise, you edit the placeholder text on a form created with the Form Page Wizard.

1 Select the New Page heading, and type **Request a Room**

The new text replaces the selected text.

2 Just above the form border, delete the text *This is an explanation of the purpose of the form...*, and type the following:

Lakewood Mountains Resort will be happy to process your room request over the Web.

3 Click the first line inside the form border just after the words *full name*. Type a comma and then type **phone number** so that the prompt now reads:

Please enter your full name, phone number, and street address:

Save

4 On the toolbar, click the Save button.

FrontPage saves your changes to the form page.

Create a form from scratch

In this exercise, you create a blank Web page and then create a form on it.

New

1 On the toolbar, click the New button.

FrontPage creates a blank Web page and displays it in Page view.

2   On the left side of the toolbar, click the Style drop-down arrow. Click Heading 1, type **Give us your suggestions**, and then press Enter.

FrontPage creates a heading for the form page and moves the insertion point to the next line.

3   On the Insert menu, point to Form, and then click Form.

FrontPage creates a form on the Web page. The form has Submit and Reset buttons.

4   Press Enter five times, and click the line below the top border of the form.

This creates space to insert form controls.

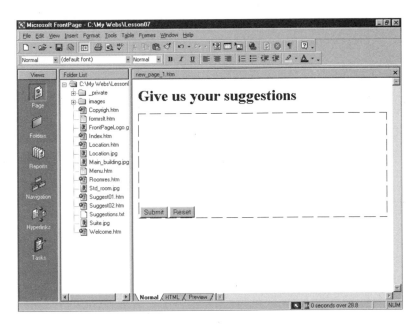

Save

5   On the toolbar, click the Save button. Type **Suggest.htm** in the File Name text box and click the Save button in the dialog box.

FrontPage saves the new form page.

Modifying Forms

Once you've created a form—whether you've used the Form Page Wizard or created the form from scratch—you can modify the form in any way you like. You can add new input fields or explanatory text, change the form properties, add new items to drop-down menus, add new check boxes or radio buttons, and change where the form data will be sent.

Add explanatory text and an input field

If you are not working through this lesson sequentially, follow the steps in "Import the Lesson 7 Practice Web" earlier in this lesson, and in the Folder List, double-click Suggest01.htm.

In this exercise, you add explanatory text and a scrolling text box to a form.

1 Click the top line inside the form border, type **We always like to hear from you!** and then press Enter.

FrontPage inserts the new text on the top line of the form.

2 Type **What's most important about a resort?** and press the Spacebar.

3 On the Insert menu, point to Form, and then click Scrolling Text Box.

FrontPage inserts a scrolling text box to the right of your question. Web site visitors will be able to enter as much text as they like in the text box.

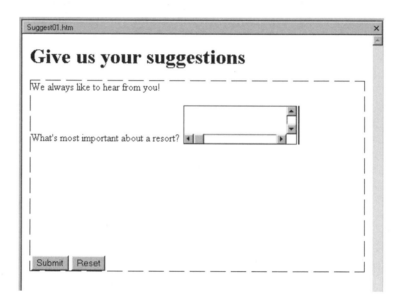

Add a drop-down menu

For a demonstration of how to add a drop-down menu to a form, in the Multimedia folder on the Microsoft FrontPage 2000 Step by Step CD-ROM, double-click the AddMenu icon.

In this exercise, you add a drop-down menu to a form.

1 Click the line under the scrolling text box, type **I really like:** and then press the Spacebar.

2 On the Insert menu, point to Form, and then click Drop-Down Menu.

FrontPage inserts a drop-down menu to the right of your new text.

3 Right-click the drop-down menu, and on the shortcut menu, click Form Field Properties.

FrontPage displays the Drop-Down Menu Properties dialog box.

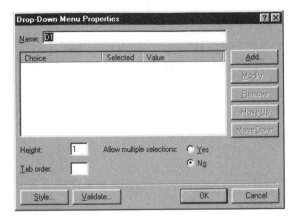

4 Click the Add button.

FrontPage displays the Add Choice dialog box. You use this dialog box to add items to the drop-down menu.

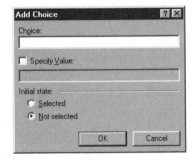

5 In the Choice text box, type **Fine food**, and then click OK.

FrontPage adds the item to the drop-down menu.

If you want one of the drop-down menu items to be selected by default, click the Selected option in the Initial State section of the Add Choice dialog box.

6 Using the same method, add Hiking, Swimming, and Snoozing to the drop-down menu.

FrontPage adds the three new items to the menu.

7 In the menu list, click Snoozing, and click the Remove button.

FrontPage removes the item from the menu list.

8 In the menu list, click Swimming, and click the Move Up button twice.

FrontPage moves Swimming to the top of the drop-down menu.

9 Click OK.

FrontPage displays the drop-down menu with its new contents on the form.

Creating Forms

You cannot open the drop-down menu in Page view. It can be opened only when the Web page is loaded or pre-viewed in a Web browser.

tip

By default, drop-down menus work the same as radio buttons; the visitor can select only one item. However, you can modify a drop-down menu to allow the visitor to select multiple items. Just right-click the drop-down menu, click Form Field Properties, and in the Drop-Down Menu Properties dialog box, click the Yes option next to Allow Multiple Selections.

Add check boxes

In this exercise, you add check boxes to the form.

❶   Click the line below the drop-down menu, type **Indoor Pastimes:** and press the Spacebar.

FrontPage moves the insertion point just to the right of your new text.

❷   On the Insert menu, point to Form, and then click Check Box.

FrontPage inserts a check box to the right of the prompt text.

❸   Type **Bingo** and press the Spacebar twice.

FrontPage inserts a label for the first check box.

❹   On the Insert menu, point to Form, click Check Box, and type **Bridge**

FrontPage inserts another check box and label.

❺   Drag the mouse to select both the word *Bridge* and the check box next to it.

The check box and its label are selected.

❻   On the Insert menu, point to Form, and then click Label.

FrontPage makes the selected text into a clickable label for the check box. Now a form user can click either the check box itself or the label to check or uncheck the check box. If you like, you can use the same method to make the word *Bingo* a clickable label.

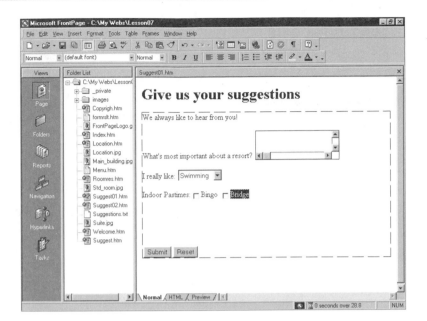

Delete form fields

In this exercise, you delete fields and their labels from a form.

1 Select the entire line containing the check boxes.

2 Press Delete.

The check boxes and text are deleted.

Save

3 On the toolbar, click the Save button.

FrontPage saves your changes.

Sending Form Data to an E-mail Address or a File

Once you have set up a form on your Web page, you need to know how to retrieve the information (the form data) entered by visitors to your Web site. By default, FrontPage sets up forms to send their data to a text file or Web page on the server. To retrieve the form data, you simply open the Web page in FrontPage. This page has the default filename of Form_results.txt.

However, you can change these defaults. You can route the form data to a different file on the Web server, to an e-mail address, to both a file and an e-mail address, to a database residing on the Web server, or to a Web server program.

Creating Forms

Send form data to an e-mail address

If you are not working through this lesson sequentially, follow the steps in "Import the Lesson 7 Practice Web" earlier in this lesson, and in the Folder List, double-click the file Suggest02.htm.

In this exercise, you route form data to your e-mail address.

important

This exercise shows the steps you perform in FrontPage to route form data to an e-mail address. However, your Web server must be configured to support this operation. Ask your system administrator or Webmaster to set it up for you.

1 Right-click a blank area of the form, and on the shortcut menu, click Form Properties.

FrontPage displays the Form Properties dialog box.

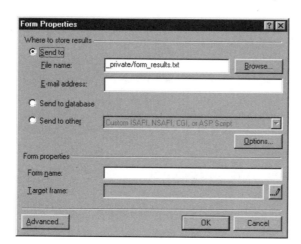

2 In the E-mail Address text box, type your own e-mail address.

If you clicked OK at this point, the form data would be sent both to a text file on the Web server and to your e-mail address.

3 Click in the File Name text box, delete the text, and then click OK.

FrontPage displays a dialog box explaining that your Web server must be configured before you can send form data to e-mail. The dialog box asks if you want to delete the e-mail address from the form.

4 Click No.

Once your Webmaster or system administrator has configured the Web server, form data will be routed to your e-mail address.

tip

FrontPage also allows you to route form data to a database or a Web server program. However, these actions require that a database or server program be set up by your Webmaster. Web server programs are often used to process and summarize large amounts of data gathered from many Web site visitors.

Send form data to a text file

In this exercise, you send form data to a text file other than the default.

1. Right-click a blank area inside the form border, and on the shortcut menu, click Form Properties.

   FrontPage displays the Form Properties dialog box.

2. In the File Name text box, delete any text currently in the text box.

3. Type **Suggestions.txt,** delete the contents of the E-mail Address text box, and click the Options button.

4. Click the File Format drop-down arrow, select Formatted Text, and click OK.

   When a Web site visitor clicks the Submit Form button, data will be sent to a file named Suggestions.txt on the Web server. If the file does not yet exist, it will be automatically created the first time a Web site visitor uses the form.

5. On the toolbar, click the Save button.

   FrontPage saves your changes.

Save

Test your form

In this exercise, you test the form you just created.

*Preview
In Browser*

1. On the toolbar, click the Preview In Browser button.

   FrontPage starts your Web browser and displays the form page.

2. In the What's Most Important text box, type **The golf course!**

3. Click the Submit button.

   Your Web browser displays a page indicating that your form will work when you publish your Web to a FrontPage-compliant Web server, as shown on the following page.

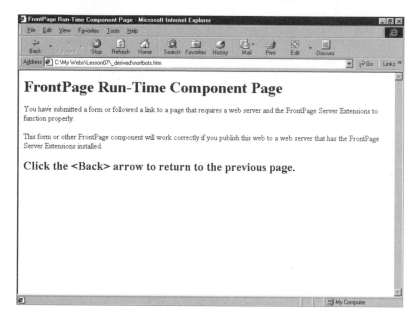

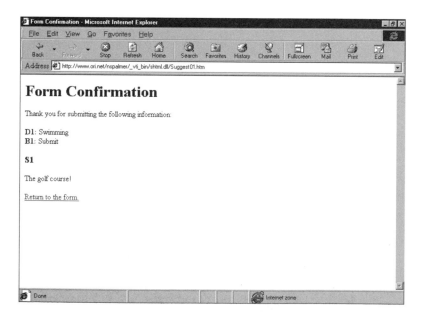

4   Click the Close button at the top-right corner of your Web browser window.

Your Web browser closes and FrontPage reappears.

After you've published your Web to a FrontPage-compliant Web server, you'll be able to test your form pages "live." When you click the Submit button, the Web server will display a confirmation page.

One Step Further **Creating a Guest Book**

One of the most popular Web site features is the Guest Book page, which allows visitors to leave their names, e-mail addresses, and comments about a Web site. FrontPage provides a template that makes it easy for you to create a guest book page for your Web site. To create a guest book page, you simply create a new Web page based on the template, and then modify the default text as you wish.

Create a guest book

In this exercise, you create a guest book page, which will allow visitors to send feedback on the Web site.

1 On the File menu, point to New, and then click Page.

FrontPage displays the New dialog box.

2 Click the Guest Book icon, and then click OK.

FrontPage creates a guest book page and displays it in Page view. Web site visitors can type their comments in the scrolling text box, and then click the Submit Comments button to send their comments to the Web server.

You can add fields to the guest book form just as you would to any other form. Position the insertion point at the desired location, and on the Insert menu, point to Form, and click the desired field.

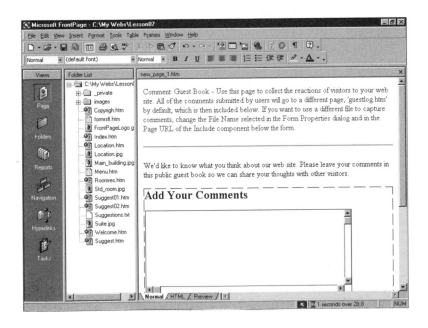

3   Select everything above the form border, and then press Enter.

FrontPage deletes the comment and the default text, and creates a blank line above the form.

4   Type **Your feedback about the Web site is welcome!**

FrontPage adds the new text above the form.

Save

5   On the toolbar, click the Save button. Type **Feedback.htm** as the filename, and click the Save button in the dialog box.

FrontPage saves your guest book page.

tip

As you've probably guessed, a guest book page is just a special kind of form. By default, the data that Web site visitors enter on the guest book page is sent to the file Guestlog.htm on the Web server. You can create a link from your home page to Guestlog.htm so that other visitors can read the comments. You can also change the data's destination in the same way as you would with any other form: by right-clicking a blank area of the form, clicking Form Properties on the shortcut menu, and using the Form Properties dialog box to specify the new destination.

Finish the lesson

1   On the File menu, click Close Web.

2   For each page, if FrontPage prompts you to save changes, click Yes.

FrontPage saves your changes and closes the Lesson07 Web.

Lesson 7 Quick Reference

To	Do this
Create a form with the Form Page Wizard	On the Views bar, click the Page icon. On the File menu, point to New, and then click Page. In the New dialog box, click the Form Page Wizard icon, click OK, and follow the wizard's instructions to add form fields. When the form is complete, click the Finish button.

Lesson 7 Quick Reference

To	Do this
Add radio buttons with the Form Page Wizard	In the Form Page Wizard dialog box, click Next, and then click the Add button. In the type of input list, click One Of Several Options. In the Edit The Prompt For This Question text box, delete the default text, type your question, and click the Next button. Type a list of radio button labels, click the Radio Buttons option, type the name of the variable to hold the data the visitor enters, and click the Next button.
Add check boxes with the Form Page Wizard	In the Form Page Wizard dialog box, click the Add button. In the type of input list, click Any Of Several Options. In the Edit The Prompt For This Question text box, delete the default text, type your question, and click the Next button. Type a list of check box labels, type the name of the variable to hold the data the visitor enters, and click the Next button.
Edit form text	Open the Web page containing the form. Add and delete text just as you normally would.
Create a form from scratch	Create or open the Web page that will contain the form, and position the insertion point at the desired location. On the Insert menu, point to Form, and then click Form.
Add a form field to a form	Open the Web page containing the form, and position the insertion point at the desired location. On the Insert menu, point to Form, and click the type of field you want to insert.
Add choices to a drop-down menu	Insert the menu on a form, right-click the menu, and click Form Field Properties. Click the Add button, add a choice, and click OK. Repeat the process to add other menu choices.
Delete a form field	Drag the mouse to select the form field and its label, and press Delete.

Lesson 7 Quick Reference

To	Do this
Change the destination of form data	Right-click a blank area of the form, click Form Properties, type the desired data destination, and click OK.
Create a guest book page	Click the Page icon on the Views bar. On the File menu, point to New, and then click Page. Click the Guest Book icon, and then click OK.

8

Using Frames

**ESTIMATED
TIME
40 min.**

In this lesson you will learn how to:

- ✔ *Design a Web site with frames.*
- ✔ *Create frames pages.*
- ✔ *Create no-frames pages.*
- ✔ *Create a front door page.*
- ✔ *Use shared borders.*

So far, everyone is pleased with your work on the Lakewood Mountains Resort Web site. You've used Microsoft FrontPage 2000 to create many impressive Web page features. But when you first planned the site back in Lesson 1, you decided that you would use frames to make the Web site easier to navigate. That feature is still on your to-do list. Both your boss and the Lakewood management are eager to see frames in action.

In this lesson, you will learn how to use frames on a Web site. You will learn how to create a frames page, how to create a contents frame, and how to create a no-frames alternative for people who either can't view frames in their Web browsers or just prefer not to. Finally, you will learn how to create frames and hyperlink menus using two of FrontPage's popular shortcuts: shared borders and navigation bars.

Import the Lesson 8 practice Web

In this exercise, you create a new Web based on the files in the Lesson08 folder in the FrontPage 2000 SBS Practice folder. You will use this Web for all the exercises in Lesson 8.

1 On the File menu, point to New, and then click Web.

FrontPage displays the New dialog box.

If your hard drive is not drive C, substitute the appropriate letter in step 2.

2 Click the Import Web Wizard icon. In the Specify The Location Of The New Web text box, type **C:\My Webs\Lesson08**, and click OK.

FrontPage displays the first Import Web Wizard dialog box.

3 Click the From A Source Directory Of Files option, click the Include Subfolders check box, and click the Browse button.

4 Browse to the Lesson08 folder in the FrontPage 2000 SBS Practice folder, and click OK.

5 Click Next twice, and then click Finish.

FrontPage creates a new Web based on the practice files and places it in the Lesson08 folder.

6 If the Folder List shows no file named Welcome.htm, right-click the file index.htm. On the shortcut menu, click Rename, type **Welcome.htm**, and press Enter.

FrontPage displays the Rename dialog box, asking if you want it to adjust hyperlinks to reflect the page's new filename.

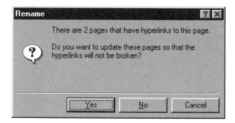

7 Click Yes.

FrontPage adjusts the hyperlinks.

Understanding Frames

Frames provide a way to divide a Web site visitor's screen into two or more areas, each of which contains a separate, independently scrolling Web page. FrontPage lets you create any of 10 different frame layouts, as shown in the Frames Pages section of the New dialog box.

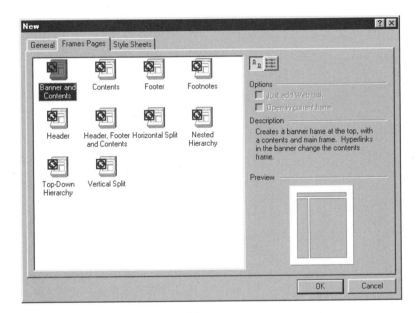

Frames earned a bad reputation when they were first introduced because they were overused and misused. Web page creators would put frames at the top of their Web sites, at the bottom, in the middle, and six ways around the ends. Web page visitors sometimes couldn't figure out what was going on.

The point of frames is to make a Web site easier, not more complicated, to view and navigate. Using too many frames or using them in ways that don't fit the content can confuse Web site visitors. A good rule of thumb is to use only as many frames as you really need. The most popular frame layout—a contents or menu frame on the left with a main frame on the right—uses only two frames. Another popular layout adds a banner frame at the top of the screen for a total of three frames. FrontPage lets you create these and eight other frame layouts.

Create a frames page

If you are not working through this lesson sequentially, follow the steps in "Import the Lesson 8 Practice Web" earlier in this lesson.

In this exercise, you create a frames page as the home page for the Lakewood Mountains Resort Web site.

1 On the Views bar, click the Page icon. On the File menu, point to New, and then click Page.

FrontPage displays the New dialog box.

2 Click the Frames Pages tab, click the Contents icon, and then click OK.

FrontPage creates a frames page and displays it in Page view.

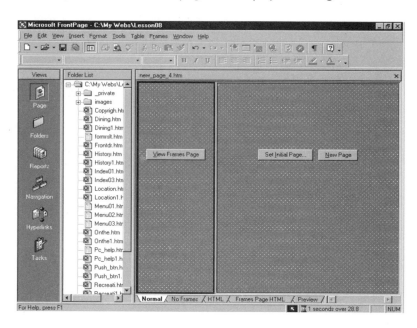

Assign Web pages to frames

For a demonstration of how to assign Web pages to frames, in the Multimedia folder on the Microsoft FrontPage 2000 Step by Step CD-ROM, double-click the Frames icon.

In this exercise, you assign Web pages to frames in the frames page, save the frames page, and then preview the frames page in your Web browser.

1 Click Set Initial Page. In the Create Hyperlink dialog box, scroll down until you see Menu01.htm, click Menu01.htm, and click OK.

FrontPage inserts the menu Web page in the contents frame on the left.

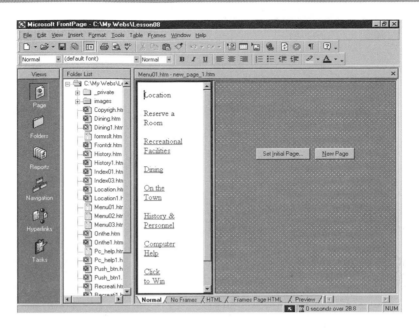

2 Click Set Initial Page again. In the Create Hyperlink dialog box, scroll down the file list until you see Welcome.htm, click Welcome.htm, and click OK.

FrontPage inserts the Welcome page in the main frame at the right.

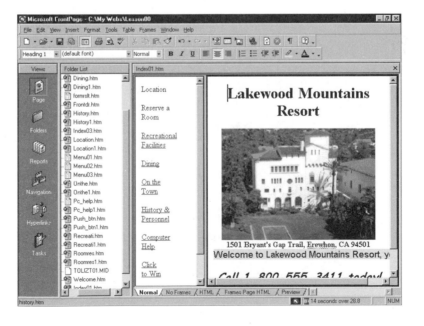

In the Save As dialog box, you can enter or change the page's title (which is different from its filename) by clicking the Change button.

Close

New

❸ On the File menu, click Save As, and then in the File Name text box, type **Index01a.htm**, and click the Save button.

FrontPage saves the frames page as the Web's home page.

❹ On the toolbar, click the Preview In Browser button.

FrontPage starts your Web browser and displays the frames page.

❺ Click the Close button at the top-right corner of your Web browser window.

Your Web browser closes and FrontPage reappears.

tip
When you're creating a frames page, you can either use existing pages to fill the frames, or you can create new pages to put in the frames. To create a new page and insert it in a frame, click the New button.

Create hyperlinks in the contents frame

In this exercise, you create hyperlinks in the contents frame and verify the result in your Web browser.

❶ In the contents frame on the left, double-click the word *Location*, right-click the selected text, and on the shortcut menu, click Hyperlink.

FrontPage displays the Create Hyperlink dialog box.

❷ Scroll down the file list, click the file Location.htm, and click OK.

FrontPage inserts the hyperlink in the selected text.

❸ In the contents frame on the left, select the text *Reserve a Room*, right-click the selected text, and on the shortcut menu, click Hyperlink.

FrontPage displays the Create Hyperlink dialog box.

❹ Scroll down the file list, click Roomres.htm, and click OK.

FrontPage inserts the hyperlink in the selected text.

Save

Preview In
Browser

❺ On the toolbar, click the Save button.

FrontPage saves the frames page, the menu page, and the main frame page with your changes.

❻ On the toolbar, click the Preview In Browser button.

FrontPage starts your Web browser and displays the frames page.

❼ In the contents frame, click the Location hyperlink.

The Lakewood Mountains Resort Location page is redisplayed in the main frame.

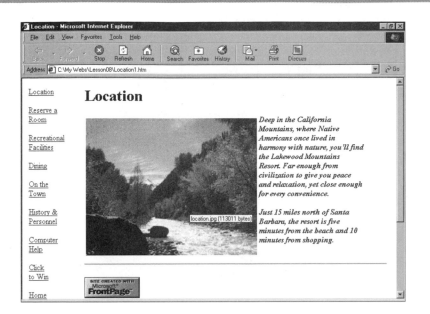

⑧   In the contents frame, click the Reserve a Room hyperlink.

The Reserve a Room page is displayed in the main frame.

⑨   Click the Close button at the top-right corner of your Web browser window.

Your Web browser closes and FrontPage reappears.

Close

Providing No-Frames Alternatives

Not everyone likes to use frames, and some older Web browsers can't display frames. For these reasons, it's wise to create a no-frames alternative for Web site visitors who either can't use frames or prefer not to do so.

There are essentially three approaches to providing a no-frames alternative for your Web site. The first is to do nothing. When you create a frames page, FrontPage creates a default no-frames page for Web site visitors whose browsers won't display frames. The page simply informs visitors that the Web site uses frames, that their browser won't display frames, and, therefore, that they are "out of luck" if they want to view the site. Because the no-frames message is all that the visitor sees, this is not a practical alternative for most serious Web sites. Certainly, you don't want Lakewood Mountains Resort to lose potential guests—even if only a small number of potential guests—just because their Web browsers won't display frames.

The second approach is to create a parallel Web hierarchy with pages that do not use frames. You then set up your Web site with a *front door* page that lets visitors select the frames or no-frames version of the Web site. This involves a certain amount of extra work, but with FrontPage, it's not as difficult as it sounds.

The third approach is somewhere in the middle. You still create a parallel hierarchy that contains no-frames versions of your Web pages. However, instead of creating a front door page, you put a no-frames version of your home page in the no-frames page that was automatically created by FrontPage. This lets visitors with older, no-frames Web browsers view your site, but does not allow visitors to choose whether they want to use frames. No-frames browsers get the no-frames Web pages; frames-capable browsers get the frames pages.

important

If you're creating a Web for a company intranet, federal law might require you to create a no-frames alternative for employees protected under the Americans with Disabilities Act (ADA).

Create a no-frames page

In this exercise, you create a no-frames home page for the Lakewood Mountains Resort Web site.

If you are not working through this lesson sequentially, follow the steps in "Import the Lesson 8 Practice Web" earlier in this lesson.

New

1 On the Views bar, click the Page icon. On the toolbar, click the New button.

FrontPage creates a new Web page and displays it in Page view.

2 On the Table menu, point to Insert, and click Table.

FrontPage displays the Insert Table dialog box.

3 Type **1** in the Rows text box, and type **100** in the Specify Width text box, if necessary. Verify that In Percent is selected, and click OK.

FrontPage inserts a two-column, one-row table on the page.

4 Verify that the insertion point is in the left table cell and on the Insert menu, click File. In the Select File dialog box, browse to the Lesson08 Web in the My Webs folder, click Menu01.htm, and then click the Open button.

FrontPage inserts the contents of the hyperlinks menu page into the left table cell. The hyperlinks, however, still point to frames pages. You will retarget the hyperlinks in the next exercise.

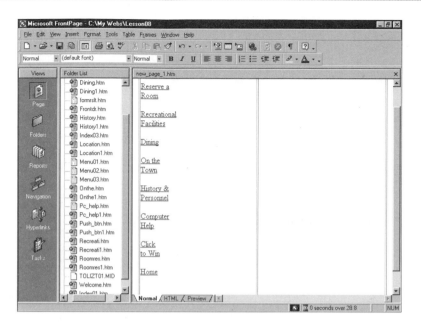

5 Use the mouse to drag the table column's right border to the left until the column is just wide enough for the longest line of hyperlink text.

6 Right-click the right column of the table, and on the shortcut menu, click Cell Properties.

FrontPage displays the Cell Properties dialog box.

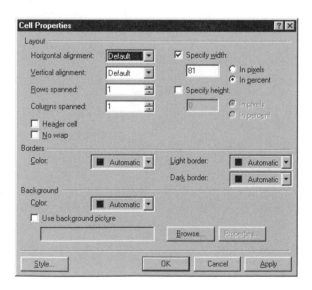

7 Click the Vertical Alignment drop-down arrow, click Top, and click OK.

FrontPage will align any content with the top of the cell.

8 On the Insert menu, click File. In the Select File dialog box, click Welcome.htm, and click the Open button.

FrontPage inserts the content of the Welcome page into the right column of the table.

9 On the File menu, click Save As to display the Save As dialog box. In the File Name text box, type **Index02.htm** and click the Save button.

FrontPage saves the no-frames home page.

Retarget hyperlinks to no-frames pages

In this exercise, you retarget hyperlinks in the no-frames page's menu column and then preview the page in your Web browser.

1 In the left column of the table, right-click the Location hyperlink, and on the shortcut menu, click Hyperlink Properties.

FrontPage displays the Edit Hyperlink dialog box.

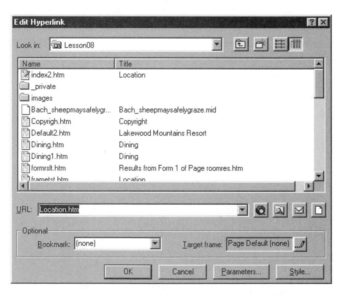

You would normally have had to create Location1.htm; in this exercise, it has been created for you.

2 In the file list, click Location1.htm, and click OK.

FrontPage retargets the hyperlink to a no-frames version of the Location Web page.

❸ Right-click the Reserve a Room hyperlink, and click Hyperlink Properties. In the Edit Hyperlink dialog box, click Roomres1.htm, and click OK.

FrontPage retargets the hyperlink to a no-frames version of the Reserve a Room page.

tip
If you wish, you can retarget the rest of the hyperlinks. The no-frames pages all end in "1.htm," such as Location1.htm, Push_btn1.htm, and so forth.

Save

Preview In Browser

❹ On the toolbar, click the Save button, and then click the Preview In Browser button.

FrontPage saves your changes and opens the page in your Web browser.

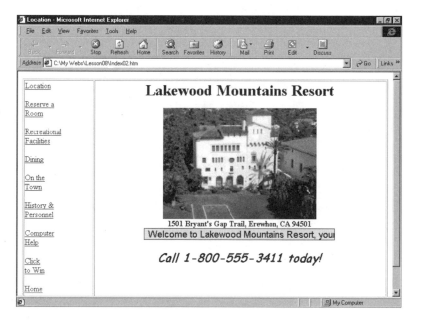

❺ Click the Location hyperlink in the left column.

Your Web browser displays Location1.htm. Notice that this page is designed so that the left column of the table displays a Web site menu, giving the appearance of a contents frame.

Close

❻ Click the Close button at the top-right corner of your Web browser window.

Your Web browser closes and FrontPage is redisplayed.

Create a front door Web page

In this exercise, you create a front door page for the Web site, which lets visitors choose whether they want to view frames or no-frames Web pages.

1 In the Folder List, double-click the file Frontdr.htm.

FrontPage displays the Frontdoor Web page in Page view. A page heading and photo have already been inserted for you.

2 Click the line below the hotel photo. On the Table menu, point to Insert, and click Table.

FrontPage displays the Insert Table dialog box.

3 Type **1** in the Rows text box, type **50** in the Specify Width text box, and click OK.

FrontPage inserts a table under the photo.

Center

4 On the Table menu, point to Select, and click Table. On the Formatting toolbar, click the Center button.

FrontPage centers the table under the photo.

5 Click in the left cell of the table, type **Use Frames**, and select the cell's text.

6 Right-click the selected text, and on the shortcut menu, click Hyperlink. In the file list, select Index01.htm, and click OK.

FrontPage inserts a hyperlink to the frames page.

7 Click in the right cell of the table, type **No Frames**, and select the cell's text.

8 Right-click the selected text and on the shortcut menu, click Hyperlink. In the file list, select Index03.htm, and click OK.

FrontPage inserts a hyperlink to the no-frames home page.

Save

9 On the toolbar, click the Save button.

FrontPage saves your changes.

Test the front door page

In this exercise, you test the front door page that lets visitors choose whether they view a frames or no-frames version of the Web site.

Preview In Browser

1 On the toolbar, click the Preview In Browser button.

FrontPage starts your Web browser.

2 Click the No Frames hyperlink.

Your Web browser displays the no-frames home page.

3 Click the Location hyperlink.

Your Web browser displays a no-frames version of the Location page.

4 Click the Web browser's Back button twice.

Your Web browser redisplays the front door page.

5 Click the Use Frames hyperlink.

Your Web browser displays the frames home page.

6 Click the Close button at the top-right corner of your Web browser window.

Your Web browser closes and FrontPage reappears.

Back

×

Close

Fill in FrontPage's default no-frames page

In this exercise, you add content to a no-frames page.

1 In the Folder List, double-click the file Index03.htm.

FrontPage displays the no-frames version of the home page in Page view.

2 On the Table menu, point to Select, and then click Table.

FrontPage selects the table containing the hyperlink menu and the home page content.

3 On the Edit menu, click Copy.

FrontPage copies the table to the Windows Clipboard.

4 In the Folder List, double-click the file Index01.htm.

FrontPage displays the frames version of the Lakewood Mountains Resort home page in Page view.

5 Click the No Frames tab at the bottom of the FrontPage window.

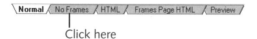

Click here

FrontPage displays the default no-frames page.

6 Select the default text. On the Edit menu, click Paste.

FrontPage deletes the default text and pastes the no-frames home page into the no-frames page.

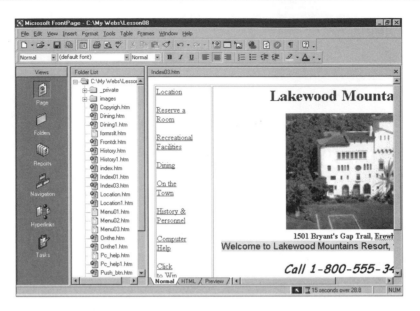

7 On the toolbar, click the Save button.

FrontPage saves your changes.

Save

<table>
<tr><td>**One Step Further**</td><td># Using Shared Borders and Navigation Bars</td></tr>
</table>

FrontPage makes it easy to create a Web site with frames, but there's an even easier method than you've seen so far. Instead of creating a frames page and assigning a page to each separate frame, you can just apply *shared borders* either to your whole Web site or to individual Web pages. A shared border is a frame that appears along the top, left, or bottom of a Web site visitor's screen. The shared border contains a FrontPage component called a *navigation bar* that automatically creates and displays hyperlinks to selected pages of your Web site.

In spite of the ease with which shared borders and navigation bars can be set up, they do have two minor disadvantages. First, navigation bars offer less flexibility than you can get if you create a frame and insert hyperlinks manually. A navigation bar will display only certain hyperlinks; you can customize it, but not much. Second, navigation bars won't work until you create a hierarchy in Navigation view—something that requires that your Web server have the FrontPage Server Extensions.

Create a Web hierarchy

If you are not working through this lesson sequentially, follow the steps in "Import the Lesson 8 Practice Web" earlier in this lesson.

In this exercise, you create a three-page Web hierarchy so that FrontPage's navigation bars will work correctly.

1 On the Views bar, click the Navigation icon.

FrontPage displays the Web in Navigation view. At present, only the home page (Welcome.htm, titled Lakewood Mountains Resort) is displayed in the Web hierarchy.

2 In the Folder List, click the file Location.htm, and drag it below the home page until a line connects it to the home page.

FrontPage inserts the Location page as a child of the home page.

3 In the Folder List, click the file Onthe.htm, and drag it below the Location page until a line connects it to the Location page.

FrontPage inserts the On the Town page as a child of the Location page.

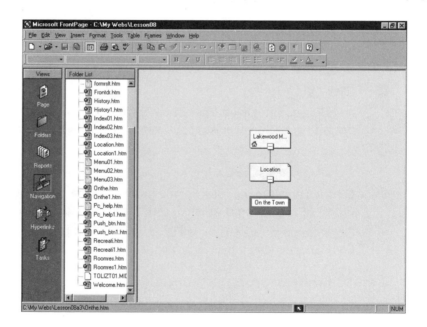

Create shared borders

In this exercise, you create shared borders for the pages in your Web hierarchy.

1 In Navigation view, double-click the Location page icon.

FrontPage opens the Location page in Page view.

2 On the Format menu, click Shared Borders.

FrontPage displays the Shared Borders dialog box.

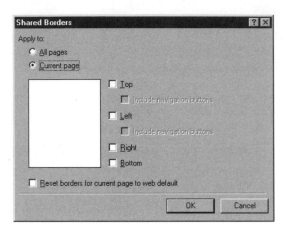

3 Make sure the Current Page option is selected, and click the Left check box to select it.

Notice that the dialog box displays a preview of the shared border layout.

4 Click OK.

FrontPage creates a left shared border for the Location page. A navigation bar with default hyperlinks appears at the top of the shared border.

5 In the Folder List, double-click the file Onthe.htm.

FrontPage opens the On the Town page in Page view.

6 On the Format menu, click Shared borders. In the dialog box, make sure the Current Page option is selected, click the Left check box, and click OK.

FrontPage creates a left shared border for the On the Town page. A navigation bar with default hyperlinks appears at the top of the shared border.

Adjust navigation bar properties

In this exercise, you will adjust navigation bar properties to include links to the home page and the On the Town page.

1 Right-click the On the Town page's navigation bar, and on the shortcut menu, click Navigation Bar Properties.

FrontPage displays the Navigation Bar Properties dialog box. Notice that the Child Level option is selected.

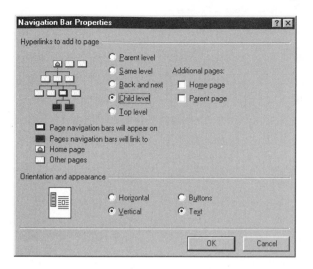

2 Click the Parent Page check box, and click the Home Page check box.

The navigation bar will include a link to the page just above the On the Town page (its "parent page") in the Web hierarchy. It will also include a link to the home page.

3 Click OK.

FrontPage adjusts the navigation bar properties. The navigation bar now shows two links: Home, leading to the home page, and Up, leading to the parent page.

Save

Close

4 On the toolbar, click the Save button, and then click the Close button at the top-right corner of the On the Town page.

FrontPage saves your changes, closes the On the Town page, and redisplays the Location page.

5 Right-click the navigation bar and click Navigation Bar Properties on the shortcut menu.

FrontPage displays the Navigation Bar Properties dialog box.

6 If necessary, click the Home Page and Parent Page check boxes, make sure the Child Level option is selected, and click OK.

The navigation bar now shows two links: Home, leading to the home page, and On the Town, leading to the On the Town page. There is no separate link for a parent page because the home page is the Location page's parent page in the Web hierarchy.

Save

7 On the toolbar, click the Save button.

FrontPage saves your changes.

Test shared borders and navigation bars

In this exercise, you test the shared borders and navigation bars in your Web browser.

Preview In Browser

1 On the toolbar, click the Preview In Browser button.

FrontPage starts your Web browser and displays the Location page. Notice the navigation bar links at the left side of the page.

Navigation —— bar links

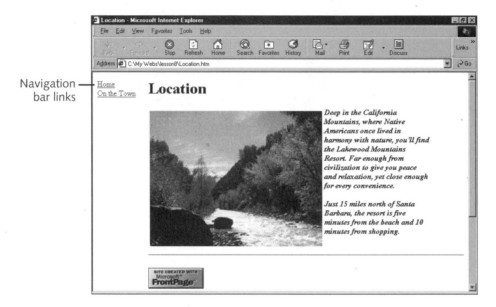

2 On the navigation bar, click the On the Town hyperlink.

Your Web browser displays the On the Town page.

3 On the navigation bar, click the Home hyperlink.

Your Web browser displays the home page.

Finish the lesson

Close

1 Click the Close button at the top-right corner of your Web browser window.

Your Web browser closes and FrontPage reappears.

2 On the File menu, click Close Web.

3 For each page, if FrontPage prompts you to save changes, click Yes.

FrontPage saves your changes and closes the Lesson08 Web.

Lesson 8 Quick Reference

To	Do this
Create a frames page	On the Views bar, click Page. On the File menu, point to New, click Page, and click the Frames Pages tab. Click the desired frame layout, and click OK.
Assign Web pages to frames	Click Set Initial Page, click the Web page to assign, and click OK. Repeat for other frames in the frames page.
Create hyperlinks in the contents frame	Type and select the text for the link, right-click the selected text, and on the shortcut menu, click Hyperlink. Click the target file, and then click OK.
Create a no-frames version of a frames page	Create a new, blank page. On the Table menu, point to Insert and click Table. Enter the appropriate number of rows and columns, set height and width, and click OK. Click in a table cell. On the Insert menu, click File, navigate to the desired folder, click the desired file, and click OK. Repeat for each table cell.
Retarget a hyperlink to a no-frames page	Right-click the hyperlink, click Hyperlink Properties, click the target file, and click OK.
Create a front door Web page	Create a new, blank page. On the new page, insert the desired content and two hyperlinks. One link should lead to the frames home page, and the other to the no-frames home page.
Fill in the default no-frames page	Display the framed home page in Page view and click the No Frames tab. Delete the default text and insert or paste the desired content.
Create shared borders and navigation bars	Click the Navigation icon on the Views bar and create a Web hierarchy. On the Format menu, click Shared Borders. Click either the All Pages or Selected Pages option, click the check box for the desired border layout, and click OK.
Adjust navigation bar properties	Display a page in Page view and right-click the navigation bar. In the dialog box, click the desired check boxes and options, and then click OK.

8

Using Frames

Review & Practice

ESTIMATED
TIME
30 min.

> **You will review and practice how to:**
>
> ✔ Create a Web page form.
> ✔ Send form data to a file or e-mail address.
> ✔ Create a guest book page.
> ✔ Create a frames page.
> ✔ Use shared borders and navigation bars.

Before you go on to Part 4, which covers publishing and maintaining your Web, you should review the skills you've learned in Part 3 by working through this Review & Practice section. You will review how to create a Web page form, route form data, create a guest book page, create a frames page, create no-frames pages, and how to use Microsoft FrontPage's shared borders feature.

Scenario

You've conducted two previous FrontPage training sessions for other account executives at Impact Public Relations. But in a coffee break after one of the sessions, a senior account executives approached you with a question. "What if you need to get information from people who visit the Web site, such as their names and addresses?"

You suggested that he come to the training session you're about to begin now. Several other people had asked about using forms and frames on a Web site, so you've got a good agenda for this class.

Step 1:   Create and Use Web Page Forms

You explain that a *form* is a way to let Web site visitors send you information, such as their names and addresses, requests for product literature, or suggestions for improving the Web site. You show how FrontPage makes it easy to create and modify forms, and how you can route form data in different ways.

1   Start FrontPage and use the One-Page Web template to create a Web.

2   Start the Form Page Wizard to create a form that gets contact information from a Web site visitor.

3   Add check boxes and radio buttons to the form.

4   Add a scrolling text box to the form.

5   Use the Guest Book template to create a guest book page.

6   Modify the default text on the guest book page.

7   Change the destination of the guest book page's data from a file on the Web server to an e-mail address.

For more information about	See
Using the One-Page Web template	Lesson 2
Using the Form Page Wizard	Lesson 7
Creating a guest book page	Lesson 7
Sending form results to an e-mail address	Lesson 7

Step 2:   Create a Frames Page

Having completed your demonstration of Web page forms, you explain that frames are a way to help visitors navigate a Web site. You show how FrontPage makes it easy to create a variety of frame layouts.

1   Display the Frames card of the New dialog box and preview five different types of frame layout.

2   Create a frames page using the Contents template.

3   Assign the Index.htm page to the main frame and create a new page for the contents frame.

4   Close your Web without saving any changes.

For more information about	See
Creating a frames page	Lesson 8
Using frame page templates	Lesson 8
Creating and editing frames pages	Lesson 8

Step 3:   **Demonstrate Shared Borders**

Now that you've shown everyone the power of frames, you're ready to show them a shortcut—FrontPage's shared borders feature, with which they can create simple frame layouts requiring minimum time and effort.

1 Use the Import Web Wizard to create a new Web based on the files in the Review03 folder of the FrontPage 2000 SBS Practice folder. Import the files into a folder named Review03 in the My Webs folder.

2 With the Web displayed in Navigation view, create a Web hierarchy with the Home page at the top, the Dining page at the second level, and both the On the Town and Recreation pages at the third level.

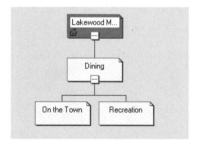

3 Add a left shared border with navigation bars to all the pages in the Web.

4 Open the Navigation Bar Properties dialog box and make the navigation bars display links to the child page, parent page, and home page.

5 Preview the Web in your Web browser and use the Navigation bars to move from the Home page to the other pages and back.

For more information about	See
Creating shared borders	Lesson 8
Setting navigation bar properties	Lesson 8
Using navigation bars	Lesson 8

Finish the Review & Practice

●   Save your changes in the Review03 practice Web and close the Web.

PART 4

Publishing and
Updating a Web

9

Publishing a Web

In this lesson you will learn how to:

✔ *Check spelling on Web pages.*

✔ *Publish a Web locally.*

✔ *Publish a Web to a Web server.*

✔ *Update a Web on a Web server.*

✔ *Maintain a Web.*

✔ *Delete a Web.*

✔ *Publish a Web to a non–FrontPage-compliant Web server.*

Publishing a Web

Your work on the Lakewood Mountains Resort Web site has been a success. Using the tools provided by Microsoft FrontPage 2000, you've created an attractive and useful set of Web pages. There's just one thing left to do: publish your Web to a Web server.

In this lesson, you will learn how to check spelling on your Web pages prior to publishing them on the Internet or on a company intranet, how to publish your Web locally to make a backup copy of your Web files, how to publish your Web to a Web server that has the FrontPage Server Extensions and to a Web server that does not, how to update and maintain your Web on the Web server, how to rename your Web, and how to delete your Web from a Web server.

Import the Lesson 9 practice Web

In this exercise, you create a new Web based on the files in the Lesson09 folder in the FrontPage 2000 SBS Practice folder. You will use this Web for all the exercises in Lesson 9.

1 On the File menu, point to New, and then click Web.

FrontPage displays the New dialog box.

If your hard disk drive has a drive letter other than C, substitute the appropriate drive letter in step 2.

2 Click the Import Web Wizard icon. In the Specify The Location Of The New Web text box, delete the default text and type **C:\My Webs\Lesson09**, and click OK.

FrontPage displays the first Import Web Wizard dialog box.

3 Click the From A Source Directory Of Files option, click the Include Subfolders check box, and click the Browse button.

4 Browse to the Lesson09 folder in the FrontPage 2000 SBS Practice folder, and click OK.

5 Click Next twice, and then click Finish.

FrontPage creates a new Web based on the practice files and places it in the Lesson09 folder.

Checking the Spelling on Web Pages

Before you publish a Web—whether on the Internet or on a company intranet—you want to make it as close to perfect as you can. Careless errors make a bad impression that extends beyond the Web site to your company itself.

At Impact Public Relations, your marketing copywriters have a saying: "No wun spels perfecly all the thyme." No matter how carefully you type information on the Web pages for Lakewood Mountains Resort, at least a few spelling errors are inevitable. To catch and correct these errors, you can use FrontPage's spelling checking feature. The spelling checker compares the words on your Web pages to the entries in its own spelling list. If FrontPage doesn't find a word in its list, it flags the word as a possible misspelling.

By default, FrontPage's spelling checker checks words as you type them on a page and underlines any words it doesn't recognize. If you like, you can correct any suspect words as soon as you see the spelling checker underline them. Because proper names and many technical terms are not included in the spelling dictionary, they are often flagged by the spelling checker. Click the Ignore button to continue checking spelling without changing the flagged word.

Most users prefer to check spelling all at once, checking a full page of text or the entire Web. In this section, you'll learn how to check spelling on an individual Web page or on your entire Web.

tip

Running a spelling check is very helpful, but it's no substitute for proofreading Web pages with your own eyes. For example, in the marketing copywriters' adage, the word *time* is misspelled as *thyme*. FrontPage's spelling checker, however, wouldn't catch that error, because *thyme* is a real word—although the wrong word in this particular context.

Check spelling on a single Web page

If you are not working through this lesson sequentially, follow the steps in "Import the Lesson 9 Practice Web" earlier in this lesson.

In this exercise, you check and correct spelling on a single page of the Lakewood Mountains Resort Web.

1 In the Folder List, double-click the file History.htm.

FrontPage displays the History and Personnel page in Page view.

2 On the Tools menu, click Spelling.

FrontPage displays the Spelling dialog box. FrontPage has flagged the word *Bromo* because the word doesn't appear in the spelling checker's word list. In this case, you know that Bromo is a proper name and is spelled correctly.

You can also press the F7 function key to check spelling.

Spelling	? X
Not in Dictionary:	Bromo
Change To:	Broom
Suggestions:	Broom / Brome / Brooms

Ignore   Ignore All
Change   Change All
Add   Suggest

Cancel

3 Click the Ignore button.

FrontPage displays the next apparent misspelling. In this case, the word *hotel* has been misspelled as *hotl*.

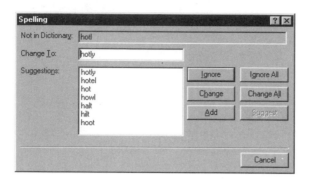

④ In the Suggestions list, click *hotel*, and then click the Change button.

FrontPage corrects the word on the Web page and displays the next apparent misspelling.

⑤ In the Suggestions list, click *problem*, and then click the Change button.

FrontPage corrects the word on the Web page and displays the next apparent misspelling. You know that *M.I.T.* is short for Massachusetts Institute of Technology, so the word is not misspelled.

⑥ Click the Ignore button.

FrontPage displays a message box stating that the spelling check is complete.

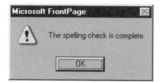

Save

⑦ On the toolbar, click the Save button.

FrontPage saves your changes.

⑧ On the File menu, click Close.

FrontPage closes the History and Personnel Web page.

tip

If you need to see a word in context to determine if it's misspelled, you can drag the Spelling dialog box to one side of the screen.

Check spelling on an entire Web

In this exercise, you check and correct spelling on the entire Lakewood Mountains Resort Web.

1   On the Views bar, click the Navigation icon, and then on the Tools menu, click Spelling.

FrontPage displays the Spelling dialog box. The Entire Web option is selected.

tip

If you want to have FrontPage locate spelling errors now, but you don't want to correct spelling until a later session, you can click the check box labeled Add A Task For Each Page With Misspellings, and then click the Start button. FrontPage will compile a list of pages with spelling errors and add them as tasks in Tasks view. When you decide to correct spelling, click the Tasks icon on the Views bar, and double-click pages that are flagged as having misspelled words.

2   Click the Start button.

FrontPage displays a list of pages with apparent spelling errors. In each row, FrontPage lists the page, the number of apparent errors on that page, and the words that seem to be misspelled.

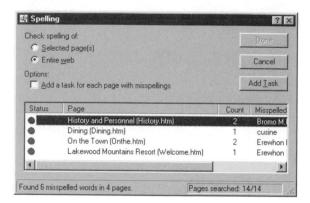

3 In the Spelling dialog box, double-click the file Dining.htm.

FrontPage displays the Dining page in Page view and flags the misspelling.

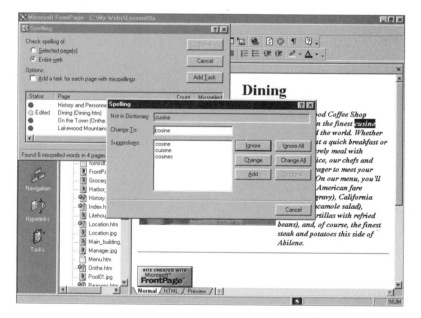

4 In the Suggestions list, click *cuisine*, and then click the Change button.

FrontPage corrects the word and displays the Continue With Next Document? dialog box, as shown on the following page.

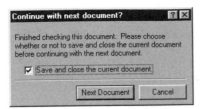

5   Click the Next Document button.

FrontPage saves your changes to the Dining page, closes the Dining page, and displays the next Web page that contains spelling errors.

6   Click the Cancel button three times to close the dialog boxes.

FrontPage ends the spelling check.

Publishing a Web

Once you've checked your Web for spelling errors, you're ready to publish it. Publishing your Web is the reason you've worked so hard to create a good looking Web in FrontPage. You should also publish a copy of your Web locally on your own hard disk drive. This local copy serves as a backup. If you make changes to your working copy of the Web (the one you will publish to a server) and then want to undo those changes, you can refer to this original copy of your Web (your locally published copy).

Before you can publish your Web, you should get the following information from your Internet Service Provider (ISP) or system administrator.

- The address of your Web server.
- The preferred home page name (index.htm or default.htm).
- The FTP server address if your Web server does not have the FrontPage Server Extensions).
- Folder information (if your Web server does not have the FrontPage Server Extensions).

Publishing a Web

Your Publishing Options

Many ISPs offer free Web hosting to their customers. To take advantage of this, you usually have to upload your Web to a subdirectory under the ISP's domain name. If your ISP's server name is isphost.com and your name is Tom Smith, for example, your Web address might be *www.isphost.com/users/tsmith*. Depending on the purpose of the Web, this might be an acceptable option. However, this approach has several drawbacks. First, free Web space is often limited to 5 MB or less—not enough for a complex Web or a business Web site. Second, you have little control over the Web address you're assigned. For a commercial Web site, it's important that the address be easy to remember and type. To create a professional Web site, it is a good idea to register your own domain name, such as ActiveEd.com or HansonBrothers.net, using your company name or some variation, and set up a business Web site with a Web hosting company that can provide the space your site will need (typically 5 MB to 100 MB).

Before you can register a domain name, you must have the following information:

- Administrative contact (information for the person who will manage the registration paperwork).

- Technical contact (information for the person who will manage and update your Web site).

- Billing contact (information for the person who will handle payment for your domain name registration and the ultimate owner of the Web).

- Server names (the primary and secondary domain names of the server that will host your Web; your ISP can provide these to you).

- Net addresses (the IP addresses for your host server names; your ISP can provide these also).

Register your domain name

These steps are subject to change.

1 Start your browser and navigate to *www.internic.net*. Click in the Search text box.

2 Type your desired domain name in the text box and press Enter. Repeat the search, trying different variations of the name, until you receive a No Match Found message.

You now have an unused domain name that you can register.

(continued)

continued

3. Make sure that your Web hosting service has mapped your domain name to their server names and net addresses.

4. Navigate to *www.internic.net* again, and click the Web Version Step-by-Step hyperlink under the Type column.

5. At the bottom of the page, click the Forms hyperlink. Enter the necessary information. Make sure the New Registration option is selected.

6. Click the Step 1: Organization Information Section button, enter the requested information, and click the Step 2: Technical Contact Information button.

7. Follow the steps to finish registering your domain name.

   InterNIC will send e-mail confirmation. Copy this information and send it to *hostmaster@internic.net*. You will be mailed a printed invoice so that you can make payment.

Publish your Web locally

If you are not working through this lesson sequentially, follow the steps in "Import the Lesson 9 Practice Web" earlier in this lesson.

In this exercise, you publish a copy of your Web to your hard disk drive on your computer.

1. On the File menu, click Publish Web.

   FrontPage displays the Publish Web dialog box.

If your hard disk has a drive letter other than C, substitute the appropriate drive letter in step 2.

2. In the Specify The Location To Publish Your Web To text box, type **C:\My Webs\Copy of Lesson09 Web**, and then click the Publish button.

   FrontPage publishes a copy of your Web to your hard disk drive and displays a message box confirming that the Web site was published successfully.

3 Click the Done button.

FrontPage closes the message box.

Publish your Web to a Web server

For a demonstration of how to publish a Web to a Web server, in the Multimedia folder on the Microsoft FrontPage 2000 Step by Step CD-ROM, double-click the Publish Web icon.

In this exercise, you publish your Web to a Web server that has FrontPage Server Extensions—what is often referred to as a *FrontPage-compliant* Web server.

important

In order to complete the following exercise, you must have access to a Web server that has the FrontPage Server Extensions. You can find a list of Web hosting services that have the FrontPage Server Extensions at *www.microsoft.saltmine.com/frontpage/wpp/list/*.

1 If necessary, connect to the Internet or to the intranet to which you'll publish your Web.

2 On the File menu, click Publish Web.

FrontPage displays the Publish Web dialog box.

To find out the URL of your Web server and the folder to which your Web is published, check with your ISP, Web hosting service, or system administrator.

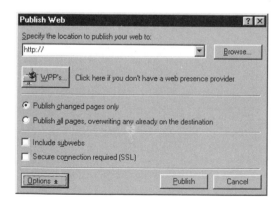

❸ In the Specify The Location To Publish Your Web To text box, type the URL of your Web server and the folder to which your Web should be published.

❹ Click the Publish button.

FrontPage connects to your Web server and for some servers, displays the Name And Password Required dialog box.

❺ If prompted, type your name in the Name text box, type your password in the Password text box, and click OK.

FrontPage publishes your Web to the selected folder of the Web server and displays a message box confirming that the Web site was published successfully.

❻ Click the Done button.

tip

On most Web servers, your user name and password are *case sensitive*, which means that the uppercase version of a letter is treated as a completely distinct letter from its lowercase counterpart. For example, if your password is *microsoft* and you type it *Microsoft*, the password will be rejected. Be sure to type your user name and password exactly as they were created for your account.

Publishing Your Web to Public Web Hosts

The number of ISPs and Web hosting services that support FrontPage is growing rapidly. (If you're not sure whether your ISP or Web hosting service has the FrontPage Server Extensions, its technical support staff can tell you.) However, some Web hosting services—especially free services—do not have the FrontPage Server Extensions.

There are two ways to publish your Web to these sites. First, you can use FTP (File Transfer Protocol), discussed later in this lesson. In many cases, however, the Web host has its own method that allows you to upload files to your folder on the Web server. GeoCities, as shown in the following figure, has a "file manager" that enables you to select files on your hard disk drive, one at a time, and upload them to your GeoCities Web folder.

You can also use the file manager to view and edit your Web page files on the server. Other public Web sites offer similar methods.

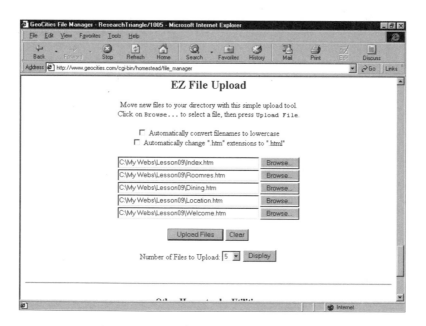

Updating and Maintaining a Web

Once you've published a Web, the job's not over. You'll continually update and improve your Web, both to enhance it with new ideas and to respond to requests from clients, such as the management of Lakewood Mountains Resort.

In this section, you will learn how to update some or all pages of your Web on a Web server, how to open a Web from the server in FrontPage, how to edit and delete your Web files on the server, how to rename your Web on the server, and how to delete your Web from the server.

Open your Web located on the Web server

To complete the following exercise, you must have published your Web to a Web server.

In this exercise, you use FrontPage to open your Web located on the remote Web server.

① On the File menu, click Open Web.

FrontPage displays the Open Web dialog box.

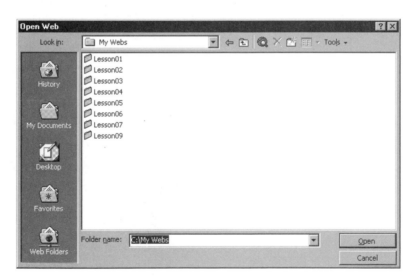

② Click the Folder Name text box, type the URL of your Web site, and then click Open.

Your Web server may prompt you for a user name and password.

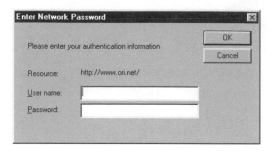

③ If prompted, type your user ID, and press Tab.

Your user or administrator ID is entered, and the insertion point moves to the Password text box.

④ If prompted, type your password, and then click OK.

FrontPage displays a list of your Web files on the Web server.

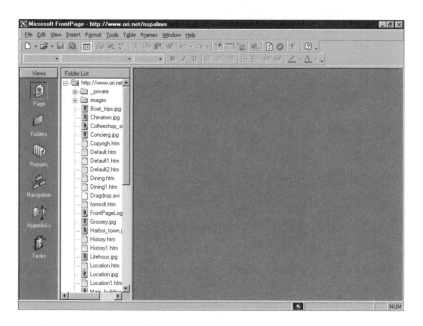

⑤ If necessary, click the file for the home page (index.htm or default.htm) and click the Open button.

FrontPage opens your home page in Page view from the Web server.

Publishing a Web   9

tip

If you are connecting to your Web server with a dial-up connection, it might take a few minutes for your home page and Web information to download to your computer. While the download is in progress, FrontPage will display the message "Requesting data" in the status bar in the lower-left corner of your screen.

When you open a file located on the Web server, FrontPage displays it in Page view, just the same as if you had opened a local copy of the file from your hard disk drive.

Maintain your Web

The Lakewood Mountains Resort manager has pointed out an error on the Web site that you need to correct. You've also found an unused video file that you want to delete to save space on the server.

In this exercise, you perform routine maintenance on your Web while it resides on the Web server.

❶ In the Folder List, double-click the file History.htm.

FrontPage downloads the page from the Web server and displays it in Page view.

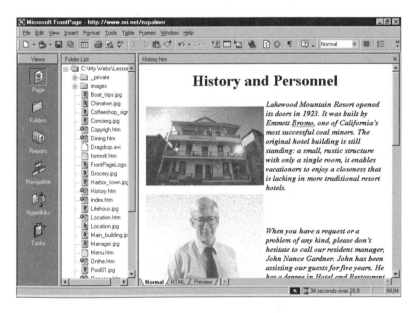

❷ In the second line of body text, click between the *2* and the *3* in *1923*.

FrontPage positions the insertion point in the text.

❸ Press the Delete key once, and then type **4**.

FrontPage changes the date of the resort's founding to 1924.

❹ On the toolbar, click the Save button.

Save

FrontPage saves your change to the History.htm file on the Web server. Because you are updating a file on the remote Web server, it takes a little longer than it would if the file were on your hard disk drive.

❺ In the Folder List, click the file Dragdrop.avi.

FrontPage selects the Dragdrop.avi file on the Web server.

❻ Press the Delete key.

FrontPage displays the Confirm Delete dialog box.

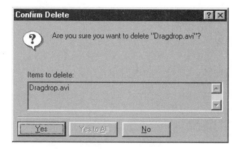

❼ Click Yes.

FrontPage deletes the file from the Web server.

Update your Web on the Web server

In this exercise, you update your Web on a Web server that has the FrontPage Server Extensions. When you update a Web, you upload new Web pages or revised versions of existing Web pages.

❶ On the File menu, click Publish Web.

FrontPage displays the Publish Web dialog box.

❷ Click the Options button.

FrontPage displays the Options section of the dialog box. Notice that the Publish Changed Pages Only option is selected. With this option selected, FrontPage will upload pages to the server only if they've been changed since they were originally published on the server.

❸ If you want to upload copies of all your Web page files, not just the ones that have changed, click the Publish All Pages option.

④ In the Specify The Location To Publish Your Web To text box, type the URL of your Web server and the folder to which your Web should be published.

⑤ Click the Publish button.

FrontPage connects to your Web server and, on some servers, displays the Name And Password Required dialog box.

If a dialog box asks whether or not to over-write a file, click Yes.

⑥ If prompted, type your name in the Name text box, type your password in the Password text box, and click OK.

FrontPage updates your Web page files on the Web server and displays a message box confirming that the Web site was published successfully.

⑦ Click the Done button.

⑧ On the File menu, click Close Web.

FrontPage closes your Web.

Rename your Web

By default, your Web name is the same as the name of the folder in which your Web is kept—whether on your local hard disk drive or on the remote Web server. For example, if your Web is in a folder named *Lakewood*, FrontPage would title your Web simply *Lakewood*. In this exercise, you rename your Web.

important

The steps for renaming a Web are the same whether you're renaming a Web on your local hard drive or on the remote Web server. However, depending on your access permissions, you might not be able to rename your Web on the Web server. Check with your system administrator if you need help.

① On the Tools menu, click Web Settings.

FrontPage displays the Web Settings dialog box.

Publishing a Web

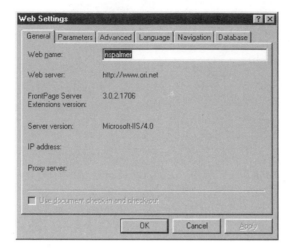

❷   In the Web Name text box, delete the default name, type **Lakewood Mountains Resort** or another new name for the Web, and click OK.

FrontPage renames your Web.

Delete your Web files from the Web server

There are two ways in which you can delete your Web from a remote Web server. First, you can delete all the files in your Web but leave the Web folder intact. Second, you can delete the files and the Web folder. You can easily delete your Web files, but it's best to leave deleting your Web folder to your Web administrator.

To delete individual files from a Web server, simply select only the files you want to delete instead of selecting all the Web files.

In this exercise, you delete your Web files from the Web server.

❶   Open your Web on the Web server using the steps described in the exercise "Open Your Web Located on the Web Server," earlier in this lesson.

FrontPage displays your Web server files in the Folder List.

❷   On the Views bar, click the Folders icon.

FrontPage displays the Web files in Folders view.

❸   On the Edit menu, click Select All.

FrontPage selects all the files in the Web folder.

❹   Press the Delete key.

FrontPage displays a dialog box asking you to confirm the deletion.

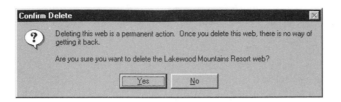

⑤ Click Yes.

FrontPage deletes the files from the Web server.

One
Step
Further **Using FTP to Upload a Web**

If your Web server does not have the FrontPage Server Extensions, FrontPage uses FTP (File Transfer Protocol) to upload your files to a server. The details of using FTP will vary depending on the Web host, but in general, you follow the same steps as if you were publishing to a Web server that has the FrontPage Server Extensions. When FrontPage connects to the Web server, it recognizes that the server does not have the FrontPage Server Extensions. After getting your user ID and password for the Web server, FrontPage prompts you to type an FTP address to which it can upload files.

Normally, you just enter the name of the Web site's FTP server, and the server automatically routes the files into your private Web folder. Though the files are uploaded to the FTP server, they will be accessible only to you.

important

The following exercise assumes you are using Internet Explorer 5 or later. If you are using an earlier version of Internet Explorer (or another Web browser that does not support FTP), you should obtain an FTP utility program. Many such programs are available on the Web from sources such as *www.download.com*. This exercise also assumes that you are uploading to a non–FrontPage-compliant Web server operated by a Web host that allows FTP uploads.

Publishing a Web

Use FTP to upload your Web files

If you are not working through this lesson sequentially, follow the steps in "Import the Lesson 9 Practice Web" earlier in this lesson.

In this exercise, you use FTP to publish your Web to a non–FrontPage-compliant Web server.

1 On the File menu, click Publish Web.

2 In the Specify The Location To Publish Your Web To text box, type the FTP address of your Web server, such as *ftp://ftp.mybigcompany.com*.

3 Click the Publish button.

FrontPage connects to the Web site's FTP server and displays a progress bar. When the connection is established, FrontPage may display the Name And Password Required dialog box.

You must begin the address with ftp:// so that FrontPage knows you want to connect to an FTP server over a network, and not simply publish your Web files locally with "ftp" as part of the Web name.

4 If prompted, in the Name text box, type your user name, and in the Password text box, type your password. Click OK.

FrontPage uploads your files to the Web host's FTP server.

---

important

Your user name and password for the FTP server might not be the same as your user name and password for the Web server. Check with your Web server's system administrator if you need help.

Finish the lesson

1 On the File menu, click Close Web.

2 For each page, if FrontPage prompts you to save changes, click Yes.

FrontPage saves your changes and closes the Lesson09 Web.

Lesson 9 Quick Reference

To	Do this
Check spelling on a Web page	In the Folder List, double-click the page you want to check, and on the Tools menu, click Spelling.
Check spelling on an entire Web	Click the Navigation icon on the Views bar. On the Tools menu, click Spelling, and click Start. Double-click pages in the page list to correct spelling.
Publish a Web locally	On the File menu, click Publish Web. In the Specify The Location To Publish Your Web To text box, type a folder name on your hard disk drive, and then click the Publish button.
Publish a Web to a FrontPage-compliant Web server	If necessary, connect to the Internet or company intranet. On the File menu, click Publish Web. In the Specify The Location To Publish Your Web To text box, type the URL of your Web server and your Web folder on the server, and click the Publish button. Type your user name and password, and then click OK.
Open a Web on a Web server	If necessary, connect to the Internet or company network. On the File menu, click Open, type the URL of your Web site, type a user name and password, and click OK.
Edit a page on a Web server	In FrontPage, open the Web on the Web server. In the Folder List, double-click the page you want to edit. In Page view, make the desired changes.
Delete a file from a Web on a Web server	In FrontPage, open the Web on the Web server. In the Folder List, click the file to delete, press the Delete key, and then click Yes.
Update a Web on a Web server	If necessary, connect to the Internet or company network. On the File menu, click Publish Web. Click Options and choose the desired update option. In the Specify The Location To Publish Your Web To text box, type the URL of the Web server and the Web folder on the server, and click the Publish button. Type your user name and password, and then click OK.
Rename a Web	On the Tools menu, click Web Settings. In the Web Name text box, delete the default text, type the new name, and click OK.

Lesson 9 Quick Reference

To	Do this
Publish a Web via FTP	In FrontPage, open a local copy of the Web and connect to the Internet or company intranet. On the File menu, click Publish Web. In the Specify The Location To Publish Your Web To text box, type **ftp://** and the URL of your FTP server, and click the Publish button. If necessary, type your user name and password, and click OK.

10

Managing and Enhancing a Web

ESTIMATED TIME
30 min.

In this lesson you will learn how to:

✔ *View reports on the status of a Web.*

✔ *Change Reports view options.*

✔ *Create and assign tasks.*

✔ *Create a table of contents.*

✔ *Animate text with dynamic HTML.*

✔ *Create page transition special effects.*

✔ *Create a search page.*

You've created and published a Web for Lakewood Mountains Resort and have received praise for your fine work with Microsoft FrontPage 2000. Now you can use FrontPage to manage and enhance the Lakewood Web.

In this lesson, you will learn how to view reports on various aspects of a FrontPage-based Web, how to change Reports view options, how to create and assign tasks for updating or enhancing the Web, how to create a table of contents for a Web site, how to animate Web page text with dynamic HTML, how to create page transition special effects, and how to create a search page.

Import the Lesson 10 practice Web

In this exercise, you create a new Web based on the files in the Lesson10 folder in the FrontPage 2000 SBS Practice folder. You will use this Web for all the exercises in Lesson 10.

❶ On the File menu, point to New, and then click Web.

FrontPage displays the New dialog box.

If your hard disk drive has a drive letter other than C, substitute the appropriate drive letter in step 2.

❷ Click the Import Web Wizard icon. In the Specify The Location Of The New Web text box, type **C:\My Webs\Lesson10**, and click OK.

FrontPage displays the first Import Web Wizard dialog box.

❸ Click the From A Source Directory Of Files option, click the Include Subfolders check box, and click the Browse button.

❹ Browse to the Lesson10 folder in the FrontPage 2000 SBS Practice folder, and click OK.

❺ Click Next twice, and click Finish.

FrontPage creates a new Web based on the practice files and places it in the Lesson10 folder.

Getting Reports on Web Status

The first step in updating or enhancing a FrontPage-based Web is to find out what needs to be updated or enhanced. To do that, FrontPage provides a Reports view that lets you display information about different aspects of your Web such as which hyperlinks are broken, which pages load more slowly than others, and so on.

Use the Reports view

**New!
2000**

In this exercise, you use the Reports view to view reports on different aspects of the Lakewood Mountains Resort Web.

If you are not working through this lesson sequentially, follow the steps in "Import the Lesson 10 Practice Web" earlier in this lesson.

❶ On the Views bar, click the Reports icon.

FrontPage displays a Site Summary report, listing the categories of reports available, the number of files covered in each category, the total size of files in each category, and a description of each category.

tip

If a floating toolbar appears over the Reports window, close it by clicking the Close button at its top-right corner.

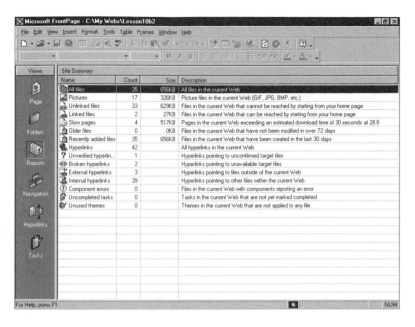

② In the Site Summary report, double-click the line for Broken Hyperlinks.

FrontPage displays a list of possibly broken hyperlinks. In this case, three hyperlinks might be broken: two lead from the Lakewood front door page (Index.htm) to Web pages that have been renamed. The third hyperlink is not broken, but because it leads to a Web page on the Internet, FrontPage cannot verify that it is not broken.

If you prefer to skip the shortcut menu, you can simply double-click the broken hyperlink to open the Edit Hyperlink dialog box.

③ Right-click the Index1.htm line, and on the shortcut menu, click Edit Hyperlink.

FrontPage displays a smaller version of the Edit Hyperlink dialog box.

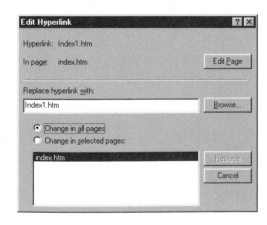

4   Click the Edit Page button.

FrontPage displays the page containing the broken hyperlink. Notice that the broken hyperlink (Use Frames) is already selected.

5   Right-click the broken hyperlink, and click Hyperlink Properties on the short-cut menu.

FrontPage displays the Edit Hyperlink dialog box.

6   Scroll down the file list, click Index01.htm, and click OK.

FrontPage repairs the broken hyperlink.

Save

7   On the toolbar, click the Save button. On the File menu, click Close, and click the Reports icon on the Views bar.

FrontPage displays the Broken Hyperlinks report. Two possibly broken hyperlinks remain.

8   On the View menu, point to Reports, and click Site Summary.

FrontPage redisplays the Site Summary report.

Change Reports view options

In this exercise, you change Reports view options by changing which files are considered "recent" and which pages are considered "slow to download." You also view the assumed speed of your Internet connection.

1   On the Tools menu, click Options.

FrontPage displays the Options dialog box.

2   Click the Reports View tab.

3 Click in the Recent Files Are Less Than text box, and type **20**.

In the Reports view, FrontPage will now list files added in the previous 19 days as Recently Added Files.

4 In the Slow Pages Take At Least text box, click the up arrow to increase the value to 40.

In the Reports view, FrontPage will now list files that take at least 40 seconds to download as slow pages.

5 Click the Assume Connection Speed Of drop-down arrow, and view the list options. Click the drop-down arrow again to close the list without changing the value.

6 Click OK.

FrontPage saves your changes.

Reports Created by FrontPage

Once you've created a Web in FrontPage, you can view reports on various aspects of your Web. The following table describes available reports.

Report	Lists
Site Summary	A summary of all available reports on the Web.
All Files	All files in the Web, with filename, title, location, size, file type, date last modified, and author.
Slow Pages	All files that take longer to load than an amount of time you specify.
Older Files	All files older than the number of days you specify.
Recently Added Files	All files added within the number of days you specify.
Recently Changed Files	All files changed within the number of days you specify.
Broken Hyperlinks	All broken or unverifiable hyperlinks.
Unlinked Files	All of the current Web's files that have no hyperlinks to or from them.

(continued)

Managing a Web

10

continued

Report	Lists
Component Errors	All FrontPage components that contain errors.
Review Status	Project status of individual pages in the Web.
Assigned To	The people to whom individual pages were assigned for updating.
Categories	Categories of Web pages if you have specified them for different types of pages in the Web.
Publish Status	Whether individual Web pages have been published to a Web server.
Uncompleted Tasks	Tasks created but not marked as completed.
Unused Themes	Themes used in the current Web but not applied to any file.

Managing FrontPage Tasks

Once you've used FrontPage's Reports view to identify the areas you'd like to update or enhance in your Web, you can use the Tasks list to track what's been done, by whom, and what still needs to be done.

To use the Tasks list, you simply click the Tasks icon on the Views bar. You can sort tasks in the Tasks list by status (Not Started or Completed), task name, the person to whom the task was assigned, priority, and date modified. You can create new tasks and edit previously created tasks. You can also create tasks from the Reports view.

Create and assign tasks

In this exercise, you create and assign tasks to members of your project team.

If you are not working through this lesson sequentially, follow the steps in "Import the Lesson 10 Practice Web" earlier in this lesson.

1. On the Views bar, click the Tasks icon.

   FrontPage displays the Tasks list. It's empty because you haven't yet created any tasks.

2. On the File menu, point to New, and then click Task.

   FrontPage displays the New Task dialog box. The Assigned To text box already has your name in it because you created the Web.

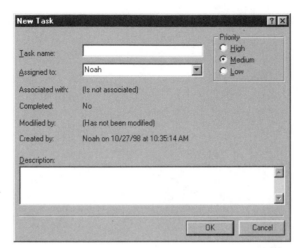

3 Click in the Task Name text box, and type **Call Lakewood re: search page**.

4 Click in the Assigned To text box, delete the default text, and type **Jim**.

You've assigned the task to Jim, a member of your project team.

5 Click in the Description text box, type **Get verbal approval from resort manager to create a search page**, and then click OK.

FrontPage creates the new task and displays it in the Tasks list. The entry shows that the task has not yet been started and displays the rest of the task information in summary form.

6 On the Views bar, click the Reports icon, and double-click the line for Broken Hyperlinks.

FrontPage displays a list of your Web's broken hyperlinks. If you have completed the exercise "Use the Reports View," earlier in this lesson, the Reports view will list only two possibly broken hyperlinks. If you have not completed the exercise, the Reports view will list three possibly broken hyperlinks.

7 Right-click the line for the index03a.htm broken hyperlink, and on the shortcut menu, click Add Task.

FrontPage displays the New Task dialog box. The task name (Fix broken hyperlink) and description (Broken URL is index3a.htm) are already filled in for you.

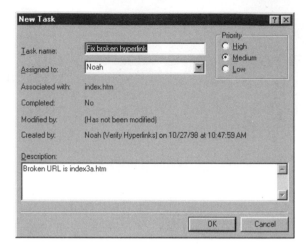

8 Click OK.

FrontPage creates a new task. In the Status column, the line for the broken hyperlink now says Added Task.

Perform a task

In this exercise, you perform a task and mark it as completed.

1 On the Views bar, click the Tasks icon.

FrontPage displays the Tasks list.

You can also right-click a task line and click Start Task on the shortcut menu.

2 Double-click the Fix Broken Hyperlink task.

FrontPage displays the Task Details dialog box.

3 Click the Start Task button.

FrontPage displays the page containing the broken hyperlink in Page view. Notice that the broken hyperlink (No Frames) is already selected.

4 Right-click the broken hyperlink, and click Hyperlink Properties on the shortcut menu.

FrontPage displays the Edit Hyperlink dialog box.

5 Scroll down the file list, click Index03.htm, and then click OK.

FrontPage repairs the broken hyperlink.

Save

6 On the toolbar, click the Save button.

FrontPage asks if you want to mark the task as completed.

7 Click Yes, on the File menu, click Close, and click the Tasks icon on the Views bar.

FrontPage displays the Tasks list. The Fix Broken Hyperlink task is now marked Completed.

8 Right-click the remaining task, *Call Lakewood,* and on the shortcut menu, click Mark As Completed.

FrontPage marks the task as completed.

Enhancing a Web

FrontPage provides scores of ways to enhance your Web—far more than can be covered here. However, three of the most popular ways to enhance a Web are to add a table of contents (which can be substituted for the links menu you created in Lesson 8), to animate text with dynamic HTML, and to create page transition special effects.

To create a table of contents, FrontPage uses its Table of Contents component. The advantage of using this component is that whenever you add a new page to your Web, the table of contents is updated automatically—unlike a standard hyperlinks menu, which you must update manually to add new hyperlinks or change old ones. The only disadvantage is that you have less control over what links are included in the table of contents than you do with a list of hyperlinks you create manually.

Text animation is another stunning set of effects that FrontPage makes as easy as clicking a few menu choices. You can animate Web page text so that it spirals into position, drops onto the page one word or one letter at a time, swoops in from the left or right, and appears with many other surprising effects.

Finally, you can create *page transitions* that control how one Web page disappears when another page loads. You can use circular or straight-line animations, make one page slide in from the left or right side over the previous page, and use other effects.

Create a table of contents

If you are not working through this lesson sequentially, follow the steps in "Import the Lesson 10 Practice Web" earlier in this lesson.

In this exercise, you create a table of contents and preview it in your Web browser.

1 On the Views bar, click the Page icon, and then click the New button on the toolbar.

FrontPage creates a new Web page and displays it in Page view.

2 On the Insert menu, point to Component, and then click Table Of Contents.

FrontPage displays the Table Of Contents Properties dialog box.

New

> ## tip
> Another way to create a table of contents is to use the Table Of Contents page template. Click the Page icon on the Views bar, point to New on the File menu, click Page, click the Table Of Contents template icon, and click OK. The result is the same as if you had inserted a Table of Contents component on a blank page.

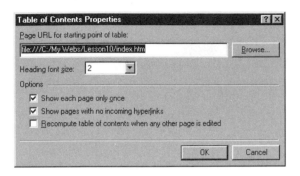

③ Click the Recompute Table Of Contents When Any Other Page Is Edited check box, and then click OK.

FrontPage inserts a Table of Contents component on the Web page.

④ Right-click a blank area of the Web page, and click Page Properties on the shortcut menu.

FrontPage displays the Page Properties dialog box.

⑤ In the Title text box, type **Table of Contents**, and then click OK.

The page's descriptive title will appear when a FrontPage user displays the Web in Folders view or when a dialog box displays a file list.

⑥ On the File menu, click Save As.

FrontPage displays the Save As dialog box.

⑦ In the File Name text box, type **Toc1.htm**, and then click the Save button.

FrontPage saves the Table of Contents page. Notice that Toc1.htm now appears in the Folder List.

*Preview
In Browser*

⑧ On the toolbar, click the Preview In Browser button.

FrontPage opens the page in your default Web browser, displaying the table of contents for the Web site. When a visitor clicks the links, he or she is taken to the corresponding pages in your Web site. Your Table of Contents page might differ from the one shown in the figure on the following page.

Managing a Web

10

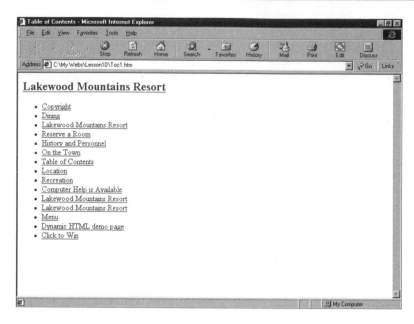

Close

9 Click the Close button at the top-right corner of your Web browser.
Your Web browser closes and FrontPage reappears.

tip

If you've created a front door page that lets users select a frames or no-frames
version of your Web, you can create a separate table of contents for each version.
Right-click the Table of Contents component, and click Table Of Contents Properties on the shortcut menu. In the Table Of Contents Properties dialog box, click
the Browse button, select the top page of the branch in the Web hierarchy, and
click OK. The table of contents will include only pages below the selected page
in the Web hierarchy—that is, pages on its particular branch of your Web.

Insert the table of contents in a contents frame

In this exercise, you insert the new table of contents into the contents frame of the home page, where it replaces the manually created hyperlinks menu.

❶   In the Folder List, double-click the file Index01.htm.

FrontPage displays the frames home page in Page view.

❷   Right-click a blank area of the menu (left) frame. On the shortcut menu, click Frame Properties.

FrontPage displays the Frame Properties dialog box.

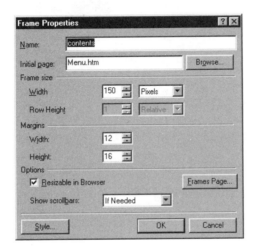

❸   Click the Browse button.

FrontPage displays the Edit Hyperlink dialog box.

❹   Scroll down the file list, click Toc1.htm, and click OK twice.

FrontPage inserts the table of contents page into the contents frame.

Save

❺   On the toolbar, click the Save button, and then click the Preview In Browser button.

Your Web browser displays the frames home page with the table of contents page in the contents frame.

*Preview
In Browser*

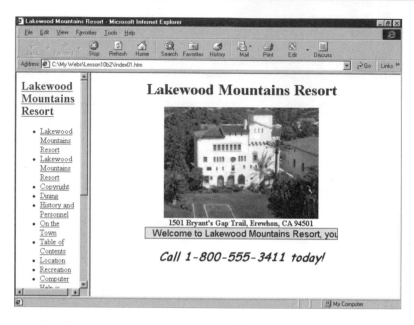

Close

⑥ Click the Close button at the top-right corner of your Web browser.

Your Web browser closes and FrontPage reappears.

Animate text with dynamic HTML

For a demonstration of how to animate text with DHTML, in the Multimedia folder on the Microsoft FrontPage 2000 Step by Step CD-ROM, double-click the Animate icon.

In this exercise, you animate text by using FrontPage's ready-to-use dynamic HTML features.

① In the Folder List, double-click the file Dhtml01.htm.

FrontPage displays the Dhtml01.htm page in Page view.

② Select the first line of text. On the Format menu, click Dynamic HTML Effects.

FrontPage displays the floating DHTML Effects toolbar.

③ Click the On drop-down arrow, and in the list, click Page Load.

The dynamic HTML effect will activate when a user loads this page into a Web browser.

④ Click the Apply drop-down arrow, and in the list, click Drop In By Word.

When the page loads in a Web browser, the text will seem to drop from above onto the page.

5 Drag the DHTML Effects toolbar out of the way if necessary, and select the second line of text.

6 On the DHTML Effects toolbar, click the On drop-down arrow, and click Mouse Over. Click the Apply drop-down arrow and click Formatting.

7 Click the Choose Settings drop-down arrow, and click Choose Font.

FrontPage displays the Font dialog box.

8 In the Font list, click Arial. In the Size text box, type **18**. Click the Color drop-down arrow, click the Red color tile on the color palette, and click OK.

9 Click the Close button at the top-right corner of the DHTML Effects toolbar. On the toolbar, click the Save button.

FrontPage closes the DHTML Effects toolbar and saves the Web page with your changes.

Close

Save

Preview dynamic HTML effects

In this exercise, you preview the animated text effects you created with dynamic HTML.

Dynamic HTML will be displayed correctly only if your browser (such as Microsoft Internet Explorer 4.0, Netscape Navigator 4.0, or later versions) supports it.

1 On the toolbar, click the Preview In Browser button.

FrontPage starts your Web browser and loads the dynamic HTML page. As the page loads, the top line of text drops into place.

2 Move the mouse pointer over the second line of text.

The text font changes to Arial, the size increases to 18 points, and the text color changes to red.

Preview In Browser

3 Move the mouse pointer away from the text.

The text changes back to its original font, size, and color.

4 Click the Close button at the top-right corner of your Web browser window.

Your Web browser closes and FrontPage reappears.

Close

Managing a Web

10

Create special transition effects

In this exercise, you create special transition effects for a Web page.

1 In the Folder List, double-click the file Index.htm.

FrontPage displays Index.htm in Page view.

2 On the Format menu, click Page Transition.

FrontPage displays the Page Transitions dialog box.

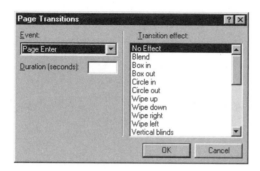

3 Click the Event drop-down arrow, and click Page Exit in the list.

The page transition effect will occur when a user exits from the selected Web page.

4 In the Duration (Seconds) text box, type **2**.

The page transition effect will last for two seconds.

5 In the Transition Effect list, click Vertical Blinds, and then click OK.

The Vertical Blinds transition effect is selected.

6 On the toolbar, click the Save button, and then click the Preview In Browser button.

7 If FrontPage displays a message box warning you that the page transition effect requires a Web browser that supports dynamic HTML, such as Internet Explorer 4.0 or higher, click OK.

FrontPage starts your Web browser and displays the selected Web page.

8 Click the Use Frames hyperlink.

As the new Web page loads, the old page disappears behind an effect that resembles opening vertical blinds on a window.

Save

*Preview
In Browser*

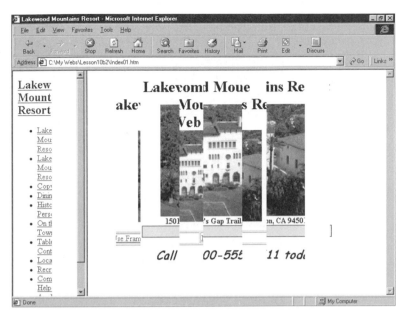

Close

9 Click the Close button at the top-right corner of your Web browser window. Your Web browser closes, and FrontPage reappears.

One Step Further

Using a Search Engine

The Lakewood Web site contains quite a few pages. Even though you've provided descriptive hyperlinks from the home page to all the other pages, some Web site visitors might want to see a list of all the pages that deal with their favorite topics or activities. FrontPage makes it easy to provide this by creating a *search page*. In a search page, Web site visitors type in a word or phrase that is likely to occur on the pages they want to see, click a Submit button, and the FrontPage-compliant Web server returns a list of all pages on the Web site that contain that word or phrase.

Of course, there's a *search engine* that looks for the relevant pages on your Web site. However, FrontPage sets up the search engine behind the scenes: you don't even need to think about it. You only need to set up the search page.

Setting up the search page itself is easy. You simply click the Page icon on the Views bar, create a new page, and select the Search Page template in the New dialog box. FrontPage creates a search page with boilerplate text that you can modify for your own needs.

Create a search page

If you are not working through this lesson sequentially, follow the steps in "Import the Lesson 10 Practice Web" earlier in this lesson.

In this exercise, you create a search page for the Lakewood Mountains Resort Web site.

❶ On the Views bar, click the Page icon.

FrontPage displays the Web in Page view.

❷ On the File menu, point to New, and then click Page.

FrontPage displays the New dialog box.

❸ Scroll down in the General pane, click the Search Page icon, and click OK.

FrontPage creates a new page using the Search Page template.

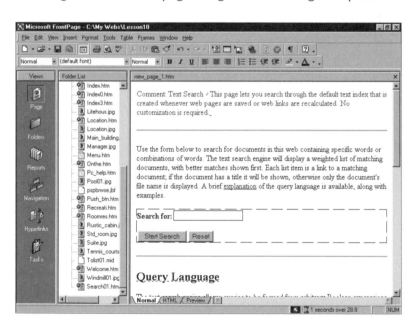

Center

Pressing Shift+Enter creates a "soft return," which allows you to retain the formatting attributes of the previous line without changing line spacing.

❹ At the top of the page, delete the comment text, and select the Heading 1 style from the Style drop-down list on the toolbar.

❺ Type **Lakewood Mountains Resort**, hold down the Shift key and press Enter, type **Search Page**, and click the Center button on the toolbar.

FrontPage creates a page heading and centers it on the page.

Center

6 Press Enter, and then click the Center button on the toolbar.

FrontPage inserts a new, left-aligned line under the heading.

7 Type **This page enables you to search for activities and services offered at Lakewood Mountains Resort**.

8 On the File menu, click Save As.

FrontPage displays the Save As dialog box.

9 In the File Name text box, type **Search01.htm**.

FrontPage enters Search01.htm as the filename for the new page.

10 Click the Change button. In the Set Page Title dialog box, type **Search this Web site** as the page title, and then click OK.

FrontPage changes the page title.

11 Click the Save button.

FrontPage saves your new search page.

Testing your search page

Because a search page is a type of form, it must be published to a FrontPage-compliant Web server in order to work. When you publish your Web—either to a separate Web server machine or on your own computer with the Microsoft Personal Web server installed—the search page will be displayed as a normal Web page form.

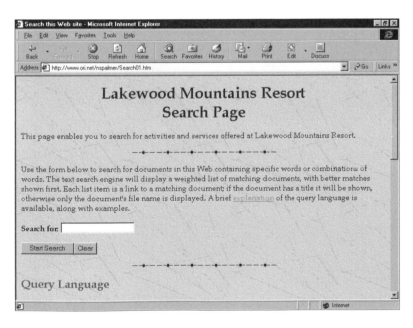

Managing a Web

10

Users of the page on your Web site simply type their desired search word(s) in the Search For text box and click the Start Search button. The Web server returns a list of the pages on your Web that contain the search word(s).

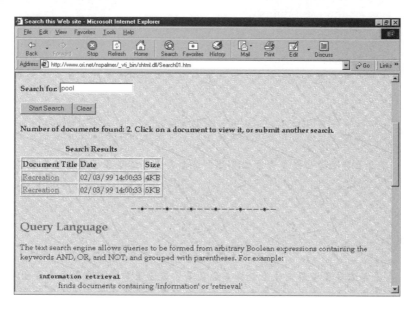

In the list, each list item is a hyperlink to the corresponding page. By clicking the hyperlink, users of your search page can display the desired page.

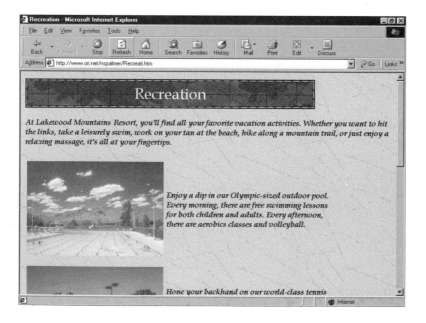

Finish the lesson

1 On the File menu, click Close Web.

2 For each page, if FrontPage prompts you to save changes, click Yes. FrontPage saves your changes and closes the Lesson10 Web.

Lesson 10 Quick Reference

To	Do this
Display a Site Summary report	Click the Reports icon on the Views bar.
Display an individual report	In the Reports view, double-click the line of the report you want to display.
Change Reports view options	On the Tools menu, click Options, click the Reports View tab, make the desired changes, and click OK.
Display the Tasks view	Click the Tasks icon on the Views bar.
Create a task	On the File menu, point to New, and then click Task. In the New Task dialog box, type a task name, description, priority, and the name of the person to whom the task is assigned. Click OK.
Complete a task	In the Tasks list, double-click the desired task, and click the Start Task button. Make the desired changes, click the Save button on the toolbar, and click Yes to mark the task as completed. *Or* right-click the task in the Tasks list, and click Mark As Completed on the shortcut menu.
Create a table of contents	In Page view, click the New button on the toolbar. On the Insert menu, point to Component, and click Table Of Contents. In the Table Of Contents Properties dialog box, make any desired changes, and then click OK. *Or* on the File menu, point to New, and then click Page. Click the Table Of Contents template icon, and click OK.
Animate text with dynamic HTML	In Page view, select the text you want to animate. On the Format menu, click Dynamic HTML Effects to display the DHTML Effects toolbar. On the toolbar, select the event to trigger the effect, the type of effect, and the settings. Click the Close button on the toolbar, save the Web page, and click the Preview In Browser button to view the animation.

Lesson 10 Quick Reference

To	Do this
Create page transition effects	Open the desired Web page in Page view. On the Format menu, click Page Transition. Select the event to trigger the effect, and specify the number of seconds the effect should last. In the Transition Effect list, click the desired effect, and click OK. On the toolbar, click the Save button, and click the Preview In Browser button to view the effect.
Create a Search page	Click the Page icon on the Views bar. On the File menu, point to New, and click Page. In the New dialog box, click the Search Page icon, and then click OK. Modify the search page as desired.

Review & Practice

**ESTIMATED
TIME
20 min.**

> **You will review and practice how to:**
>
> ✔ *Check spelling on a Web.*
> ✔ *Publish a Web to a Web server.*
> ✔ *Update a Web on a Web server.*
> ✔ *View reports on Web status.*
> ✔ *Change Reports view options.*
> ✔ *Use the Tasks list.*
> ✔ *Animate text with dynamic HTML.*
> ✔ *Create a search form.*

Congratulations! You've finished all the lessons in *Microsoft FrontPage 2000 Step by Step*. You've learned how to create a Web, and how to enhance Web pages with themes, multimedia, and FrontPage components. You've learned how to create a Web structure and insert hyperlinks that let users navigate a Web. You've learned how to get user feedback by creating Web page forms. You've also learned how to publish and update a Web on a Web server.

Before you go on to your own Web design work, you should review the skills you've learned in Part 4 by working through this Review & Practice section. You will review how to check spelling, publish and update your Web on a Web server, use the Reports and Tasks views, animate text by using dynamic HTML, create page transition effects, and create a search page.

Scenario

Your boss at Impact Public Relations wants all the account executives to be able to do Web work for clients. She's asked you to conduct one more training session and teach your coworkers how to publish a Web on a Web server.

Step 1:   Check a Web

You explain that before you publish a Web to a Web server, you should always check it for accuracy and completeness. At a minimum, that means making sure there are no spelling errors in the Web and that all the Web pages are finished. You show how FrontPage's features make it quick and easy.

❶   Create a Web based on the files in the Review04 folder in the FrontPage 2000 SBS Practice folder.

❷   Display the practice Web in Navigation view, and check the spelling on all pages in the Web. Check spelling on an individual page.

❸   View different types of reports in the Reports view.

❹   Display the Tasks list, and add a task. Complete the task, and mark it as completed.

For more information about	See
Checking spelling	Lesson 9
Using the Reports view	Lesson 10
Using the Tasks view	Lesson 10
Adding a task	Lesson 10
Marking a task as completed	Lesson 10

Step 2:   Publish a Web

Once you've checked a Web, the next step is to publish it. You explain that FrontPage can publish a Web to a Web server, automatically creating all the necessary files and folders. However, you warn, some Web servers do not support FrontPage's features, so occasionally you might be required to publish the files via FTP.

❶   Back up the Review04 practice Web by publishing a copy to your computer's hard disk drive.

❷   Publish the Review04 practice Web to your folder on a FrontPage-compliant Web server.

❸ Publish a Web to a server that is not FrontPage-compliant.

❹ Update your Web on a Web server by publishing only new and changed files in your Web.

For more information about	See
Backing up your Web	Lesson 9
Publishing to a FrontPage-compliant Web server	Lesson 9
Publishing to a non–FrontPage-compliant Web server	Lesson 9

Step 3: Update and Maintain a Web

When you first design a Web, you work with local Web page files on your computer's hard disk. However, even after a Web is published on a Web server, you can add new files, publish updated versions of existing files, and make other changes in the Web.

❶ Open your Web on the Web server, and delete the files Dining.htm and Coffeeshop_sign.jpg.

❷ Add a page transition effect to your home page on the Web server.

❸ Create a search form page, add it to your Web on the Web server, and update the Menu.htm page by adding a hyperlink to the search form.

❹ Use dynamic HTML to animate the text *Lakewood Mountains Resort* on the page Welcome.htm.

For more information about	See
Opening a Web on a Web server	Lesson 9
Deleting a file on a Web server	Lesson 9
Publishing a new file to your Web	Lesson 9
Creating a search form	Lesson 10
Animating text with dynamic HTML	Lesson 10

Finish the Review & Practice

❶ Save changes to your Web files and disconnect from the Web server.

❷ Quit FrontPage.

A

Upgrading
from FrontPage 98

Microsoft FrontPage 2000 has many new features that make it easier for you to create Web pages and Web sites. Because you might need a little help making the transition from FrontPage 98 to FrontPage 2000, this appendix walks you through the most important issues that you face when you upgrade.

Replacing FrontPage 98 with FrontPage 2000

You don't need to uninstall FrontPage 98 before you install FrontPage 2000. In fact, it's much better if you *don't* uninstall FrontPage 98. When you install FrontPage 2000 on top of your old installation of FrontPage 98, the setup program will keep all of your settings and preferences from the previous version and use them in FrontPage 2000.

If you want to run FrontPage 2000 and keep your installation of FrontPage 98, you simply install FrontPage 2000 in a folder different from the one in which you have FrontPage 98.

Using FrontPage 98 Webs in FrontPage 2000

In the lessons of this book, you import Web files from the book's CD-ROM and create new FrontPage-based Webs with the imported files. To accomplish that, you use the Import Web Wizard. Note that if a set of Web files used a theme or had a Web page navigation hierarchy, those are not preserved when you import the files to create a Web.

When you create a Web in FrontPage (whether you use FrontPage 2000 or FrontPage 98), information about the Web theme, hierarchy, and other features is stored in the Microsoft Windows folder on your hard disk drive. You had to import Webs from the CD because the Web information wasn't on your hard disk drive. But when you install FrontPage 2000 on the same computer as your previous copy of FrontPage, the Web information is just where it ought to be. As a result, you can start using your existing Webs from FrontPage 98 as soon as you install FrontPage 2000.

Getting to Know FrontPage 2000's New Features

FrontPage 2000 has many new features that make it easier to design attractive, interactive Web sites. Navigation is easier, there are more ready-to-use components, and it is easy to integrate databases and spreadsheets into Web pages.

FrontPage 2000 also offers new themes, as well as the ability to modify existing themes or create your own. You can insert Microsoft Excel 2000 worksheets, PivotTables, and charts on Web pages, as well as a variety of new FrontPage components. It's easier to write and edit HTML and Web page script code.

Interface Changes

The FrontPage Editor and FrontPage Explorer are now integrated into a single program, as are many other features. The user interface changes are summarized in the table.

FrontPage 98	FrontPage 2000
FrontPage Editor and FrontPage Explorer	No longer separate programs. Integrated into a single FrontPage program.
All Files view	Integrated into the Folders view.
Hyperlink Status view	Integrated into the Reports view.
Themes view	Themes now accessed in a dialog box from the Format menu.

Ease of Use

FrontPage 2000 is designed to be even easier to use than FrontPage 98. Apart from the interface changes already discussed, FrontPage is now designed to look and work just like the other programs in Microsoft Office 2000—with the same themes, toolbars, menus, and shortcuts, as well as tools such as the Format Painter (familiar to users of Microsoft Word), HTML help, and background spelling checking. Some of the most important ease of use features are summarized in the table.

Ease of use feature	Explanation
Web themes	More themes (over 60) that are easier to apply, either to entire Webs or to individual pages.
Format Painter	FrontPage users can now copy the formatting from one block of text to another by positioning the mouse pointer on the text with the desired format, clicking the toolbar's Format Painter button, and selecting the text to be formatted.
Spelling checker	Spelling checking can now be done in the background as you type. If you prefer, it can still be done in a single operation as in FrontPage 98.
Personalized menus	Menu choices used most often are prominently placed on each menu, or menus can be expanded to display all menu choices. Menus also expand automatically as needed.
Personalized toolbars	Toolbars share screen space with each other based on how frequently they are used. When a toolbar is used often, it is "promoted" to occupy more screen space.
Customizable toolbars	Toolbars are easier to customize by dragging buttons.
HTML help	HTML help is now available while users work in FrontPage.
Answer Wizard	Users can ask questions in plain language and get the information they need.

Web Page Design

FrontPage includes many new features that make it easier to design attractive and functional Web pages. There are more themes than before, and it's easier to customize themes or create your own. With or without themes, it's now easier to customize color schemes of your Web pages. There's improved support for Cascading Style Sheets (CSS), and you can position items in exact locations on your Web pages. Finally, there are more ready-to-use FrontPage components that build features into your Web pages. The table summarizes some of the most important new features for Web page design.

Web page design feature	Explanation
Web themes	More themes (over 60) that are easier to apply, either to entire Webs or to individual Web pages.
Customized themes	Now easier to modify existing themes or create your own.
Color tools	Now easier to apply colors to graphics and text or use a color picker to select custom colors. Entire color schemes can be selected either by selecting a theme or by picking a custom color scheme from the color wheel.
Pixel precise positioning	Now you can place page elements in exact locations with relative or absolute positioning.
Cascading Style Sheets (CSS)	Improved support for Cascading Style Sheets, following the CSS2 standard.
More FrontPage components	New components include Category, Spreadsheet, PivotTable, and Chart.

Web Page Coding

If you're an advanced Web page designer, FrontPage now gives you more power and flexibility to write and customize your Web page code—whether it's HTML, DHTML, script code, XML, or ASP. Web page coding features are summarized in the table.

Web page coding feature	Explanation
HTML source code preservation	FrontPage 2000 does not modify the HTML code you write or insert, so you can write your own code or even import code from other Web tools. FrontPage even preserves tag and comment order, capitalization, and white space.
Quickly insert code in HTML view	Buttons and drop-down menus now make it easier to insert code directly on a Web page displayed in HTML view.
Personalized HTML formatting	You can now customize how you want your code indented, what colors tags should use, what to capitalize, and when optional tags are to be used. Your preferences are automatically applied to any new or imported HTML code.

Web page coding feature	Explanation
Reveal tags in WYSIWYG (What You See Is What You Get) view	With a page displayed in Normal view, you can select Reveal Tags to show which HTML tags are producing certain effects.
Edit code directly	With a page displayed in HTML view, it's now easier to edit HTML, DHTML, script code, XML, and ASP.
Microsoft Script Editor	You can now edit and debug scripts written in VBScript or JavaScript using the Microsoft Script Editor, which is a separate program on the Macro submenu of the Tools menu.

Web Publishing

FrontPage 2000 adds and improves several features that make it easier for you to publish and update your Webs on the Internet or on an intranet. You now have better control over publishing individual Web pages to update your Web site; you can create Webs in FrontPage without needing a Web server; and you can more easily publish your Webs to Web servers that don't have the FrontPage Server Extensions. The Web publishing improvements are summarized in the following table.

Web publishing feature	Explanation
Page-level control	You can now decide which pages to upload to the Web server by marking specific pages as "do not publish" or by choosing to publish only pages that have changed.
Create Webs anywhere	You can now create and test a Web on your computer without a Web server connection.
Publish Webs anywhere	You can more easily publish to non–FrontPage-compliant Web servers by using FrontPage's built-in FTP feature.
Progress Indicator	When you publish your Web, a progress indicator shows how much of the Web remains to be published.

B

Features that Require the FrontPage Server Extensions

In an ideal situation, you develop a Web site in FrontPage and publish it to a Web server that has the FrontPage Server Extensions. However, if you don't have access to a FrontPage-compliant Web server, some features you create in FrontPage won't work.

Understanding FrontPage-Specific Features

There are two categories of features that require the FrontPage Server Extensions to work properly. The first category consists of *run-time components*. When Web pages are loaded into a browser, these components interact with the Web server. If the Web server isn't set up to work with FrontPage components, the components won't function properly.

Run-time component	Explanation
Confirmation field	Confirms the data a user enters in a form field.
Default form handler	Sends form data to a Web page file.
Hit Counter component	Counts and displays the number of times a page has been viewed by Web site visitors.
Registration component	Registers Web site visitors to create a members-only Web site.
Scheduled Include Page component	Inserts one Web page in another Web page at a specified time.
Scheduled Picture component	Inserts an image on a Web page at a specified time.
Search component	Inserts a search form on a Web page.

The second category consists of components that depend on extra Web information that is stored by FrontPage—in particular, information about the Web hierarchy that you can create in Navigation view. These components won't work because the server doesn't store and provide that information as needed.

Navigational component	Explanation
Navigation bar	Displays hyperlinks in shared borders.
Page Banner component	Displays the page title at the top of the page.
Table of Contents component	Creates and displays a Web site table of contents.

Using Workarounds for FrontPage Components

Navigational components are the easiest components to replace with Web page workarounds.

Navigational component	Replace with
Navigation bars	Manually created hyperlinks.
Page Banner component	Text page heading (use Heading 1 style).
Table of Contents component	A page of hyperlinks in a menu frame.

Run-time components can often be replaced by components designed for the specific non-FrontPage Web server to which you're publishing your Web. For example, the popular GeoCities Web site has its own hit counter, guest book, and other components that you can download. You can then use FrontPage to incorporate these components into your Web pages and upload them (manually, of course) to the Web site.

C

If You're New to Windows

If you are new to Microsoft Windows, this appendix will show you the basics you need to get started. You'll get an overview of Windows features, and you'll learn how to use online Help to answer your questions and find out more about using the Windows operating systems.

If You're New to Windows

Windows is an easy-to-use computer environment that helps you handle the daily work that you perform with your computer. You can use Windows 95, Windows 98, or Windows NT to run Microsoft FrontPage—the explanations in this appendix are included for all of these operating systems.

The way you use Windows 95, Windows 98, Windows NT, and programs designed for these operating systems is similar. The programs look much alike, and you use similar menus to tell them what to do. In this section, you'll learn how to operate the basic program.

Start Windows

Starting Windows is as easy as turning on your computer.

❶　If your computer isn't on, turn it on now.

❷　If you are using Windows NT, press Ctrl+Alt+Del to display a dialog box asking for your user name and password. If you are using Windows 95 or Windows 98, you will see this dialog box if your computer is connected to a network.

❸　Type your user name and password in the appropriate boxes, and click OK.

　　If you don't know your user name or password, contact your system administrator for assistance.

Close

4 If you see the Welcome dialog box, click the Close button. Your screen should look similar to the following illustration.

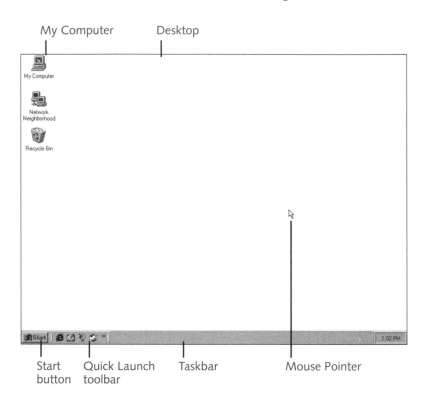

Using the Mouse

Although you can use the keyboard for most actions, many actions are easier to do using a *mouse*. The mouse controls a pointer on the screen, as shown in the above illustration. You move the pointer by sliding the mouse over a flat surface in the direction you want the pointer to move. If you run out of room to move the mouse, lift it up and then put it down in another location.

important

In this book, we assume that your mouse is set up so that the left button is the primary button and the right button is the secondary button. If your mouse is configured the opposite way, for left-handed use, use the right button when we tell you to use the left, and vice versa.

You'll use five basic mouse actions throughout this book.

When you are directed to	Do this
Point to an item	Move the mouse to place the pointer over the item.
Click an item	Point to the item on your screen, and quickly press and release the left mouse button.
Right-click an item	Point to the item on your screen, and then quickly press and release the right mouse button. Clicking the right mouse button often displays a shortcut menu with a list of command choices that apply to that item.
Double-click an item	Point to the item, and then quickly press and release the left mouse button twice.
Drag an item	Point to an item, and then hold down the left mouse button as you move the pointer. Once the item is moved to the appropriate location, release the left mouse button.

Using Window Controls

All programs designed for Windows have common elements that you use to scroll, size, move, and close a window.

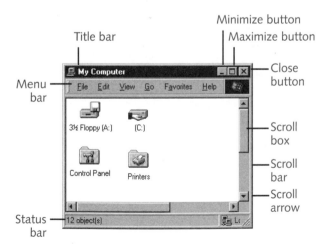

To	Do this	Button
Move, or *scroll*, vertically or horizontally through the contents of a window that extends beyond the screen	Click a scroll bar or scroll arrow, or drag the scroll box. The previous illustration identifies these screen elements.	
Enlarge a window to fill the screen	Click the Maximize button, or double-click the window title bar.	▢
Restore a window to its previous size	Click the Restore button, or double-click the window title bar. When a window is maximized, the Maximize button changes to the Restore button.	▣
Reduce a window to a button on the Windows taskbar	Click the Minimize button. To display a minimized window, click its button on the Windows taskbar.	▬
Move a window	Drag the window title bar.	
Close a window	Click the Close button.	✕

Using Menus

Just like a restaurant menu, a program menu provides a list of options from which you can choose. On program menus, these options are called *commands*. To select a menu or a menu command, click the item you want.

tip

You can also use the keyboard to make menu selections. Press the Alt key to activate the menu bar, press the key that corresponds to the highlighted or underlined letter of the menu name, and then press the key that corresponds to the highlighted or underlined letter of the command name.

In the following exercise, you'll open and make selections from a menu.

Open and make selections from a menu

❶ On the desktop, double-click the My Computer icon.

The My Computer window opens.

You can also press Alt+E to open the Edit menu.

❷ In the My Computer window, on the menu bar, click Edit.

The Edit menu appears. Some commands are disabled; this means they aren't available.

Your screen should look similar to the following illustration.

Command is not available

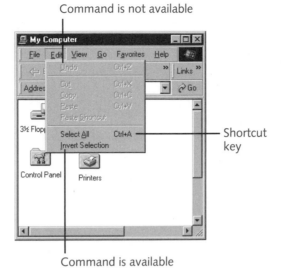

Shortcut
key

Command is available

❸ Click Edit again to close the menu.

❹ On the menu bar, click View to open the View menu.

❺ On the View menu, click Status Bar if there isn't a check mark beside it. Then click View again.

Your screen should look similar to the following illustration.

A check mark means that multiple items within a group can be simultaneously selected. A bullet means that only one item can be selected.

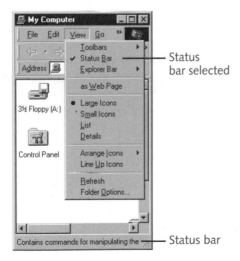

Status
bar selected

Status bar

❻ On the View menu, click Status Bar again.

The menu closes, and the status bar is no longer displayed.

Your screen should look similar to the following illustration.

Status bar inactive

A right-point-ing arrow appearing after a command name means that additional commands are available.

7 On the View menu, click Status Bar again.

The status bar is displayed.

8 On the View menu, point to Arrange Icons.

A submenu listing additional menu choices appears.

9 Click By Drive Letter.

The icons representing the drives on your computer are arranged alphabeti-cally by drive letter.

Close

10 In the upper-right corner of the My Computer window, click the Close button to close the window.

tip

If you do a lot of typing, you might want to learn the key combinations for com-mands you use frequently. Pressing the key combination is a quick way to acti-vate a command. If a key combination is available for a command, it is listed to the right of the command name on the menu. For example, on the Edit menu, Ctrl+C is listed as the key combination for the Copy command.

Using Dialog Boxes

When you choose a command name that is followed by an ellipsis (...), a dialog box appears so that you can provide more information about how the command should be carried out. Dialog boxes have standard features, as shown in the following illustration.

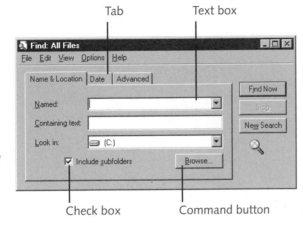

Tab   Text box

You can also use the keyboard to select the item by holding down Alt as you press the underlined letter.

Check box   Command button

To enter text in a text box, click inside the box and begin typing. Or you can press the Tab key to move around the dialog box.

Display the Taskbar Properties dialog box

Some dialog boxes provide several categories of options displayed on separate tabs. In this exercise, you customize the list of programs that appears on your Start menu.

❶ On the Windows taskbar, click the Start button.

The Start menu appears.

❷ On the Start menu, point to Settings. In Windows 95 and NT, click Taskbar. In Windows 98, click Taskbar & Start Menu.

The Taskbar Properties dialog box appears.

Click the top of an obscured tab to make it visible.

❸ In the Taskbar Properties dialog box, click the Start Menu Programs tab to make it active.

❹ Click the Taskbar Options tab, and then select the Show Small Icons In Start Menu check box.

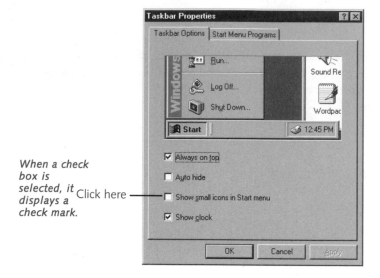

When a check box is selected, it displays a check mark. Click here ——

5 Clear the check box, and then select it again; be sure to watch how the display in the dialog box changes.

Clearing a check box will turn off the option, and selecting a check box will turn on the option.

6 Click the Cancel button.

The dialog box closes without changing any settings.

Getting Help with Windows

When you're at work and you have a question, you might ask a coworker or consult a reference book. To find out more about functions and features in Windows, you can use the Help system. Using Windows Help is one of the quickest, most efficient ways to find your answer. You can access Windows Help from the Start menu. For Help specific to a program, such as FrontPage 2000, each Windows program also includes its own Help system.

After the Help window opens, you can choose one of three ways to best research your question. To find instructions about broad categories, you can look on the Contents tab. Or you can search the Help index to find information about specific topics. Finally, you can look on the last tab (in Windows 95 and Windows NT, the Find tab; in Windows 98, the Search tab) to search the Help files based on keywords that you provide. The Help topics are short and concise, so you can get the exact information you need quickly. There are also shortcut icons in many Help topics that you can use to directly go to or to perform the task you want or to list Related Topics.

In Windows 98, on the Help toolbar, click Web Help to automatically connect to Microsoft's Support Online Web site. Once connected, you can expand your search to include the Microsoft Knowledge Base, Troubleshooting Wizards, Newsgroups, and downloadable files. Just follow the directions on the screen.

Viewing Help Contents

The Contents tab is organized like a book's table of contents. As you choose top-level topics, called *chapters*, you see a list of more detailed subtopics from which to choose.

Find Help about general categories

Suppose you want to see what documents you've chosen to print. In this exercise, you look up Windows Help instructions for finding out this information.

Windows 95 and NT

1   On the Windows taskbar, click Start, and then click Help.

The Help Topics window appears.

2   If necessary, click the Contents tab to make it active.

3   Double-click How To.

The icon changes to an open book, and a set of subtopics appears.

4   Double-click Print.

More subtopics appear.

5   Double-click Viewing Documents Waiting To Be Printed.

A Help window appears.

6   In Windows 95, to see a definition of *print queue,* click the underlined words.

A pop-up window containing the definition of the term appears.

7   Click anywhere outside that window to close it.

8   In both Windows 95 and Windows NT, read the information about viewing documents in the print queue, and then close Help.

Windows 98

1   On the Windows taskbar, click Start, and then click Help.

The Windows Help window appears.

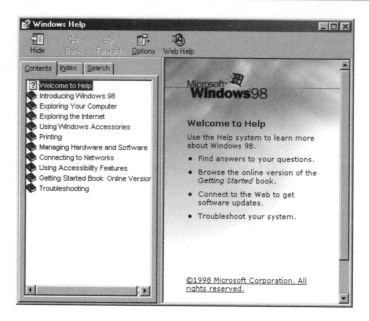

② If necessary, click the Contents tab to make it active.

③ Click Printing.

The icon changes to an open book, and a set of subtopics appears.

④ Click View A List Of Documents Waiting To Be Printed.

The topic appears in the right frame of the Windows Help window.

⑤ To see a definition of *print queue,* in the right frame, click the underlined words.

A pop-up window containing the definition of the term appears.

⑥ Click anywhere outside that window to close it.

⑦ Read the information about viewing documents in the print queue, and then close Windows Help.

Finding Help About Specific Topics

The two remaining tabs in the Windows Help window allow you to find specific Help topics. The Index tab is organized like a book's index. Keywords for topics are organized alphabetically. You can either type the keyword you want to find or scroll through the list of keywords. You can then select from one or more topic choices.

On the Find or Search tab, you can also enter a keyword. The main difference between these two tabs is that you get a list of all Help topics in which that keyword appears, not just the topics that begin with that word.

Find specific Help topics by using the Help index

In this exercise, you use the Help index to learn how to print help topics.

Windows 95

1 On the Windows taskbar, click Start, and then click Help.
The Help Topics window appears.

2 Click the Index tab to make it active.

3 In the text box, type **printing**
A list of printing-related topics appears.

4 In that list, click Help Information, Printing A Copy Of, and click Display.
The Windows Help window appears.

5 Read the information, and then close Windows Help.

Windows NT

1 On the Windows taskbar, click Start, and then click Help.
The Windows NT Help window appears.

2 Click the Index tab to make it active.

3 In the text box, type **printing**
A list of printing-related topics appears.

4 In that list, click Help Topics, and then click Display.
The Windows NT Help window appears.

5 Read the Help topic, and then close Windows Help.

Windows 98

1 On the Windows taskbar, click Start, and then click Help.
The Windows Help window appears.

2 Click the Index tab to make it active.

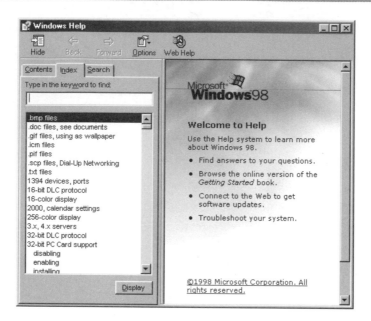

③   In the Type In The Keywords To Find box, type **printing**

A list of printing-related topics appears.

④   In that list, click Help Topics, and then click Display.

The topic is displayed in the frame on the right side of the Help window.

⑤   Click the underlined word, *frame*.

A pop-up window containing an explanation of the term appears.

⑥   Click anywhere outside that window to close it.

⑦   Read the information about printing Help topics, and close Windows Help.

Find specific Help topics by using the Find or Search tab

In this exercise, you use the Find or Search tab to learn how to print a document.

Windows 95

①   On the Windows taskbar, click Start, and then click Help.

The Help window appears.

②   Click the Find tab to make it active.

③   If you are using Find for the first time, the Find Setup Wizard dialog box appears. Click Next, and then click Finish to complete and close the wizard.

The wizard creates a search index for your Help files. This might take a few minutes.

❹ In the text box, type **print**

All printing-related topics are displayed in the third list box.

❺ In the Click A Topic Then Click Display list, scroll down, click Printing A Document, and then click Display.

The Windows Help window appears.

❻ Read the information about printing a document, and close Windows Help.

Windows NT

❶ On the Windows taskbar, click Start, and then click Help.

The Windows NT Help window appears.

❷ Click the Find tab to make it active.

❸ If the Find Setup Wizard appears, click Next, and then click Finish to complete and close the wizard.

The wizard creates a search index for your Help files. This might take a few minutes.

❹ In the text box, type **printing**

All printing-related topics are displayed in the third list box.

❺ In the Click A Topic Then Click Display list, scroll down, click To Print A Document, and then click Display.

The Windows NT Help window appears.

❻ Read the information about printing a document, and then close Windows NT Help.

Windows 98

❶ On the Windows taskbar, click Start, and then click Help.

The Windows Help window appears.

❷ Click the Search tab to make it active.

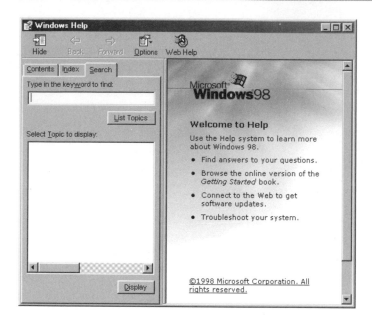

❸ In the Type In The Keyword To Find box, type **print** and click List Topics.

A list of print-related topics is displayed in the Select Topic To Display list box.

❹ In the Select Topic To Display list box, scroll down, click To Print A Document, and then click Display.

The topic is displayed in the right frame of the Windows Help window.

❺ Read the information about printing a document, and close Windows Help.

Find Help in a dialog box

Almost every dialog box includes a question mark–shaped Help button in the upper-right corner of its window. When you click this button and then click any dialog box item, a Help window appears that explains what the item is and how to use it. In this exercise, you'll get help in a dialog box.

❶ On the Windows taskbar, click Start, and then click Run.

The Run dialog box appears.

❷ Click the Help button.

The mouse pointer changes to an arrow with a question mark.

❸ Click the Open text box.

A pop-up window providing information about how to use the Open text box appears.

❹ Click anywhere outside the Help window to close it.

The mouse pointer returns to its previous shape.

❺ Close the Run dialog box.

---

tip

Windows NT and Windows 95 users can change the way the Help topics appear on the screen. In any Help topic window, click Options, point to Font, and then click a font size option to change the size of the text.

Quit Windows

Close

❶ If you are finished using Windows, close any open windows by clicking the Close button in each window.

❷ On the Windows taskbar, click Start, and then click Shut Down.

The Shut Down Windows window appears.

Windows 95

❸ Be sure the Shut Down The Computer option is selected, and then click Yes.

A message indicates that it is now safe to turn off your computer.

Windows 98

❸ Be sure the Shut Down option is selected, and then click OK.

A message indicates that it is now safe to turn off your computer.

---

important

To avoid loss of data or damage to your operating system, always quit Windows by using the Shut Down command on the Start menu before you turn off your computer.

Windows NT

❸ Be sure the Shut Down The Computer option is selected, and then click Yes.

A message indicates that it is now safe to turn off your computer.

Index

ActiveEducation & Microsoft Press

Microsoft FrontPage 2000 Step by Step has been created by the professional trainers and writers at ActiveEducation, Inc., to the exacting standards you've come to expect from Microsoft Press. Together, we are pleased to present this self-paced training guide, which you can use individually or as part of a class.

ActiveEducation creates top-quality information technology training content that teaches essential computer skills for today's workplace. ActiveEducation courses are designed to provide the most effective training available and to help people become more productive computer users. Each ActiveEducation course, including this Step by Step book, undergoes rigorous quality control, instructional design, and technical review procedures to ensure that the course is instructionally and technically superior in content and approach. ActiveEducation (*www.activeeducation.com*) courses are available in book form and on the Internet.

Microsoft Press is the book publishing division of Microsoft Corporation, the leading publisher of information about Microsoft products and services. Microsoft Press is dedicated to providing the highest quality computer books and multimedia training and reference tools that make using Microsoft software easier, more enjoyable, and more productive.

About the Author

Scott Palmer has worked in the computer industry for 18 years—almost since its inception. As a programmer, author, and teacher, he has written about computer technology for *The Wall Street Journal, USA Today, InfoWorld, PC World, PC Techniques, Government Computer News*, and many other publications. A former distinguished teacher at Indiana University, he has been teaching people to use computers since 1981. Currently he conducts computer training, programs, and consults. He is the author of 15 computer books.

MICROSOFT LICENSE AGREEMENT
Book Companion CD

IMPORTANT—READ CAREFULLY: This Microsoft End-User License Agreement ("EULA") is a legal agreement between you (either an individual or an entity) and Microsoft Corporation for the Microsoft product identified above, which includes computer software and may include associated media, printed materials, and "online" or electronic documentation ("SOFTWARE PRODUCT"). Any component included within the SOFTWARE PRODUCT that is accompanied by a separate End-User License Agreement shall be governed by such agreement and not the terms set forth below. By installing, copying, or otherwise using the SOFTWARE PRODUCT, you agree to be bound by the terms of this EULA. If you do not agree to the terms of this EULA, you are not authorized to install, copy, or otherwise use the SOFTWARE PRODUCT; you may, however, return the SOFTWARE PRODUCT, along with all printed materials and other items that form a part of the Microsoft product that includes the SOFTWARE PRODUCT, to the place you obtained them for a full refund.

SOFTWARE PRODUCT LICENSE

The SOFTWARE PRODUCT is protected by United States copyright laws and international copyright treaties, as well as other intellectual property laws and treaties. The SOFTWARE PRODUCT is licensed, not sold.

1. **GRANT OF LICENSE.** This EULA grants you the following rights:

   a. **Software Product.** You may install and use one copy of the SOFTWARE PRODUCT on a single computer. The primary user of the computer on which the SOFTWARE PRODUCT is installed may make a second copy for his or her exclusive use on a portable computer.

   b. **Storage/Network Use.** You may also store or install a copy of the SOFTWARE PRODUCT on a storage device, such as a network server, used only to install or run the SOFTWARE PRODUCT on your other computers over an internal network; however, you must acquire and dedicate a license for each separate computer on which the SOFTWARE PRODUCT is installed or run from the storage device. A license for the SOFTWARE PRODUCT may not be shared or used concurrently on different computers.

   c. **License Pak.** If you have acquired this EULA in a Microsoft License Pak, you may make the number of additional copies of the computer software portion of the SOFTWARE PRODUCT authorized on the printed copy of this EULA, and you may use each copy in the manner specified above. You are also entitled to make a corresponding number of secondary copies for portable computer use as specified above.

   d. **Sample Code.** Solely with respect to portions, if any, of the SOFTWARE PRODUCT that are identified within the SOFTWARE PRODUCT as sample code (the "SAMPLE CODE"):

      i. **Use and Modification.** Microsoft grants you the right to use and modify the source code version of the SAMPLE CODE, *provided* you comply with subsection (d)(iii) below. You may not distribute the SAMPLE CODE, or any modified version of the SAMPLE CODE, in source code form.

      ii. **Redistributable Files.** Provided you comply with subsection (d)(iii) below, Microsoft grants you a nonexclusive, royalty-free right to reproduce and distribute the object code version of the SAMPLE CODE and of any modified SAMPLE CODE, other than SAMPLE CODE, or any modified version thereof, designated as not redistributable in the Readme file that forms a part of the SOFTWARE PRODUCT (the "Non-Redistributable Sample Code"). All SAMPLE CODE other than the Non-Redistributable Sample Code is collectively referred to as the "REDISTRIBUTABLES."

      iii. **Redistribution Requirements.** If you redistribute the REDISTRIBUTABLES, you agree to: (i) distribute the REDISTRIBUTABLES in object code form only in conjunction with and as a part of your software application product; (ii) not use Microsoft's name, logo, or trademarks to market your software application product; (iii) include a valid copyright notice on your software application product; (iv) indemnify, hold harmless, and defend Microsoft from and against any claims or lawsuits, including attorney's fees, that arise or result from the use or distribution of your software application product; and (v) not permit further distribution of the REDISTRIBUTABLES by your end user. Contact Microsoft for the applicable royalties due and other licensing terms for all other uses and/or distribution of the REDISTRIBUTABLES.

2. **DESCRIPTION OF OTHER RIGHTS AND LIMITATIONS.**

   - **Limitations on Reverse Engineering, Decompilation, and Disassembly.** You may not reverse engineer, decompile, or disassemble the SOFTWARE PRODUCT, except and only to the extent that such activity is expressly permitted by applicable law notwithstanding this limitation.

   - **Separation of Components.** The SOFTWARE PRODUCT is licensed as a single product. Its component parts may not be separated for use on more than one computer.

   - **Rental.** You may not rent, lease, or lend the SOFTWARE PRODUCT.

   - **Support Services.** Microsoft may, but is not obligated to, provide you with support services related to the SOFTWARE PRODUCT ("Support Services"). Use of Support Services is governed by the Microsoft policies and programs described in the user manual, in "online" documentation, and/or other Microsoft-provided materials. Any supplemental software code provided to you as part of the Support Services shall be considered part of the SOFTWARE PRODUCT and subject to the terms and conditions of this EULA. With respect to technical information you provide to Microsoft as part of the Support Services, Microsoft may use such information for its business purposes, including for product support and development. Microsoft will not utilize such technical information in a form that personally identifies you.

- **Software Transfer.** You may permanently transfer all of your rights under this EULA, provided you retain no copies, you transfer all of the SOFTWARE PRODUCT (including all component parts, the media and printed materials, any upgrades, this EULA, and, if applicable, the Certificate of Authenticity), **and** the recipient agrees to the terms of this EULA.

- **Termination.** Without prejudice to any other rights, Microsoft may terminate this EULA if you fail to comply with the terms and conditions of this EULA. In such event, you must destroy all copies of the SOFTWARE PRODUCT and all of its component parts.

3. **COPYRIGHT.** All title and copyrights in and to the SOFTWARE PRODUCT (including but not limited to any images, photographs, animations, video, audio, music, text, SAMPLE CODE, REDISTRIBUTABLES, and "applets" incorporated into the SOFTWARE PRODUCT) and any copies of the SOFTWARE PRODUCT are owned by Microsoft or its suppliers. The SOFTWARE PRODUCT is protected by copyright laws and international treaty provisions. Therefore, you must treat the SOFTWARE PRODUCT like any other copyrighted material **except** that you may install the SOFTWARE PRODUCT on a single computer provided you keep the original solely for backup or archival purposes. You may not copy the printed materials accompanying the SOFTWARE PRODUCT.

4. **U.S. GOVERNMENT RESTRICTED RIGHTS.** The SOFTWARE PRODUCT and documentation are provided with RESTRICTED RIGHTS. Use, duplication, or disclosure by the Government is subject to restrictions as set forth in subparagraph (c)(1)(ii) of the Rights in Technical Data and Computer Software clause at DFARS 252.227-7013 or subparagraphs (c)(1) and (2) of the Commercial Computer Software—Restricted Rights at 48 CFR 52.227-19, as applicable. Manufacturer is Microsoft Corporation/One Microsoft Way/Redmond, WA 98052-6399.

5. **EXPORT RESTRICTIONS.** You agree that you will not export or re-export the SOFTWARE PRODUCT, any part thereof, or any process or service that is the direct product of the SOFTWARE PRODUCT (the foregoing collectively referred to as the "Restricted Components"), to any country, person, entity, or end user subject to U.S. export restrictions. You specifically agree not to export or re-export any of the Restricted Components (i) to any country to which the U.S. has embargoed or restricted the export of goods or services, which currently include, but are not necessarily limited to Cuba, Iran, Iraq, Libya, North Korea, Sudan, and Syria, or to any national of any such country, wherever located, who intends to transmit or transport the Restricted Components back to such country; (ii) to any end-user who you know or have reason to know will utilize the Restricted Components in the design, development, or production of nuclear, chemical, or biological weapons; or (iii) to any end-user who has been prohibited from participating in U.S. export transactions by any federal agency of the U.S. government. You warrant and represent that neither the BXA nor any other U.S. federal agency has suspended, revoked, or denied your export privileges.

DISCLAIMER OF WARRANTY

NO WARRANTIES OR CONDITIONS. MICROSOFT EXPRESSLY DISCLAIMS ANY WARRANTY OR CONDITION FOR THE SOFTWARE PRODUCT. THE SOFTWARE PRODUCT AND ANY RELATED DOCUMENTATION IS PROVIDED "AS IS" WITHOUT WARRANTY OR CONDITION OF ANY KIND, EITHER EXPRESS OR IMPLIED, INCLUDING, WITHOUT LIMITATION, THE IMPLIED WARRANTIES OF MERCHANTABILITY, FITNESS FOR A PARTICULAR PURPOSE, OR NONINFRINGEMENT. THE ENTIRE RISK ARISING OUT OF USE OR PERFORMANCE OF THE SOFTWARE PRODUCT REMAINS WITH YOU.

LIMITATION OF LIABILITY. TO THE MAXIMUM EXTENT PERMITTED BY APPLICABLE LAW, IN NO EVENT SHALL MICROSOFT OR ITS SUPPLIERS BE LIABLE FOR ANY SPECIAL, INCIDENTAL, INDIRECT, OR CONSEQUENTIAL DAMAGES WHATSOEVER (INCLUDING, WITHOUT LIMITATION, DAMAGES FOR LOSS OF BUSINESS PROFITS, BUSINESS INTERRUPTION, LOSS OF BUSINESS INFORMATION, OR ANY OTHER PECUNIARY LOSS) ARISING OUT OF THE USE OF OR INABILITY TO USE THE SOFTWARE PRODUCT OR THE PROVISION OF OR FAILURE TO PROVIDE SUPPORT SERVICES, EVEN IF MICROSOFT HAS BEEN ADVISED OF THE POSSIBILITY OF SUCH DAMAGES. IN ANY CASE, MICROSOFT'S ENTIRE LIABILITY UNDER ANY PROVISION OF THIS EULA SHALL BE LIMITED TO THE GREATER OF THE AMOUNT ACTUALLY PAID BY YOU FOR THE SOFTWARE PRODUCT OR US$5.00; PROVIDED HOWEVER, IF YOU HAVE ENTERED INTO A MICROSOFT SUPPORT SERVICES AGREEMENT, MICROSOFT'S ENTIRE LIABILITY REGARDING SUPPORT SERVICES SHALL BE GOVERNED BY THE TERMS OF THAT AGREEMENT. BECAUSE SOME STATES AND JURISDICTIONS DO NOT ALLOW THE EXCLUSION OR LIMITATION OF LIABILITY, THE ABOVE LIMITATION MAY NOT APPLY TO YOU.

MISCELLANEOUS

This EULA is governed by the laws of the State of Washington USA, except and only to the extent that applicable law mandates governing law of a different jurisdiction.

Should you have any questions concerning this EULA, or if you desire to contact Microsoft for any reason, please contact the Microsoft subsidiary serving your country, or write: Microsoft Sales Information Center/One Microsoft Way/Redmond, WA 98052-6399.

PN 097-0002296

Microsoft®

FrontPage 2000
Step by Step CD-ROM

The enclosed CD-ROM contains ready-to-use practice files that complement the lessons in this book as well as the FrontPage 2000 software. To use the CD, you'll need either the Windows 95, Windows 98, or the Windows NT version 4 operating system.

Before you begin the Step by Step lessons, read the "Using the Microsoft FrontPage 2000 Step by Step CD-ROM" section of this book. There you'll find detailed information about the contents of the CD and easy instructions telling you how to install the files on your computer's hard disk.

Please take a few moments to read the License Agreement on the previous page before using the enclosed CD.